WHERE
ARE THE
MEN?

WHERE ARE THE MEN?

---
712 PLACES
YOU HAVEN'T THOUGHT TO LOOK

BOBBIE MOSTYN

InData Group, Inc.

Published by:
InData Group, Inc.
1420 NW Gilman Blvd., Box 2313
Issaquah, WA 98027

ISBN 0-9673969-0-5

Library of Congress CCN 99-95481

Printed in the United States of America
First Printing: August 1999

Cover design by Michael Mostyn

Where are the Men? website:

www.wherearethemen.com

To my husband and soul mate, Mike . . .
I'm so glad I found you!

ACKNOWLEDGMENTS

My husband, Mike,
for his continued support and encouragement . . .
I couldn't have done it without you!

My dear friend, Sally Pearce,
for her invaluable insight and wisdom,
but most of all, for the wonderful friendship
and laughs we've shared.

The sage advice of my friend and mentor, Mitzi,
who helped me see the light.

A special thanks to Gloria Flynn . . .
for her help and support.

And to all those men who unknowingly
contributed to the success of
Where Are The Men?

CONTENTS

INTRODUCTION / 13

PART 1
PREPARATION

1 IS ANYONE OUT THERE? / 17
WHERE DO I LOOK?
SUCCESS IS IN THE "POP!"

2 PARTICIPATE / 25
WHAT'S GOING ON?
BE OBSERVANT
FIND OPPORTUNITIES

3 BE OUTGOING / 31
TALK TO THEM
CULTIVATE FRIENDSHIPS
CAN YOU BELIEVE HE TALKED TO ME?
UNCOMFORTABLE SITUATIONS
APPROACHING A GROUP

4 PERSEVERE / 41
FIND THE TIME
KEEP AT IT
MOTIVATION . . . IT'S UP TO YOU!

5 IT'S YOUR CHOICE / 47
TRY SOMETHING DIFFERENT
BE OPEN TO ALL OPPORTUNITIES

6 FINAL THOUGHTS / 53
AFFIRMATIONS AND VISUALIZATION
HOW DO I KNOW HE'S NOT A WACKO?
FINDING MONEY
ARE YOU READY?

**PART 2
OPPORTUNITIES**

7 WHERE THEY WORK AND LIVE / 59
THE WORKPLACE
THE HOME FRONT

8 WHERE THEY SPEND THEIR LEISURE / 81
CAR STUFF
HIGH FLYERS
THEIR HOBBIES
THEY GOTTA HAVE MUSIC
THEY ARE GAMBLERS
GROUP INVOLVEMENT
LEARN SOMETHING NEW
COMPUTERS AND THE NET
VOLUNTEERING
THE POLITICAL ARENA

9 WHERE THEY RECREATE / 105
PARTICIPATION SPORTS
WINTER ACTIVITIES
SPECTATOR SPORTS
BOATING AND WATER SPORTS
FISHING
THE OUTDOOR SPORTSMAN

10   WHERE THEY SHOP / 131
BUILDING SUPPLIES
OUTDOORS AND SPORTING GOODS
HIGH-QUALITY STUFF
NOSTALGIA
OTHER SHOPPING OPPORTUNITIES

11   WHERE THEY TRAVEL / 141
TRANSPORTATION
LODGING
WEEKEND GETAWAYS
DESTINATION IDEAS

12   GOING OUT ALONE / 153
DINING ALONE
AFTER HOURS

13   GETTING PEOPLE TOGETHER / 165
LET'S HAVE A PARTY
ORGANIZE FUN ACTIVITIES

14   AND IF THAT'S NOT ENOUGH / 175
EVENINGS AND WEEKENDS
MORE PLACES MEN FREQUENT
THINGS TO DO WITH KIDS
DOG DAYS
START A SMALL BUSINESS
SERVICES MEN USE
SERENDIPITY

15   FOR SENIORS ONLY / 201
LIVING ARRANGEMENTS
LEISURE ACTIVITIES
RECREATION
TRAVELING
SERENDIPITY

AFTERWARD / 221

INTRODUCTION

According to recent government estimates, there are more than 75 million single people in the U.S. and out of every one hundred unattached people, forty-six are men. However, on closer investigation we find some startling statistics when these figures are broken down into age groups.

For example, if we look at one hundred singles, aged 25 to 44, we find fifty-four are male. If we then pair these fellows with the females, we'll have forty-six couples and eight men without a partner.

Surprised?

Unfortunately, this male surplus does not last long. Let's look at the next set of singles, aged 45 to 64. In this group of a hundred, when we pair the guys with the gals, we end up with forty couples and twenty females by themselves.

But it gets worse. By the time we reach the "65 and over" crowd, *fifty* women will be without a partner!

And so it is, with some urgency, I write *Where are the Men?* Simply put, this is a book about where to find men and ways to meet them. In the following pages I will let you in on many of the creative ways I have discovered for meeting single males . . . where they are plentiful and ways to position yourself to interact with them. You will become aware of the many options available for mingling with a variety of men . . . where to shop, have fun and relax, as you get involved in a whole new realm of opportunities. You will, also, be given suggestions for places to go when you are by yourself, ideas to help you locate well-to-do bachelors and, for the mature woman, hints on where to meet retired gentlemen.

If you are looking for a how-to on keeping a man or developing successful relationships . . . this is not it. You would be better served if that were left to the experts. But if you are one of the millions of single women who has ever asked, "Where are the men?" . . . you need to look no further. It is ten years in the making and filled with more than 700 suggestions for meeting eligible fellows of all ages, many tried and true, and others where you'll wonder, "Why didn't I think of that?"

There is an old Chinese adage, "Give a man a fish and he will eat for a day, teach a man to fish and he will eat for the rest of his life."

Think of *Where are the Men?* as your manual on fishing – knowing the best way to find them and how to get their attention. It is your guide to the multitude of choices and opportunities you have to be around men and ways to interact with them. Glean from it as much as possible, as you embark on what may be the most important and rewarding "fishing" expedition in your life . . . finding the man of your dreams.

I know it is possible . . . you see, I found mine and so will you!

PART 1

PREPARATION

*"An archer cannot hit the bullseye
if he doesn't know where the target is."*
– Anonymous

1

IS ANYONE OUT THERE?

By the time my thirtieth birthday came around, I was a mess. I was lonely, depressed and struggling with my self-esteem (on a scale of one to ten, I was a one). And all because the man who vowed to "love, honor and obey, 'til death do us part" decided he could not keep his promise.

It had not been a pretty picture, but since most of you are well acquainted with the many challenges facing the newly divorced, I will spare you further details regarding mine. Let me just say, it took considerable time and effort to get through it, but it was now time to get on with my life, and more importantly, to start dating.

Not knowing what else to do, I reluctantly ventured into the singles realm, spending countless evenings with "the girls" and hitting more singles bars than I'd care to remember. Unfortunately, not only did I not meet any interesting men, I didn't like it very much. (I found it very demeaning . . . the anticipation of someone approaching you, waiting for validation of your self-worth by whether or not *he* chooses to talk to you. Some people handle this very well, but not me.)

As the dateless months slowly passed, I began to realize, much to my chagrin, my knight in shining armor was not going to be knocking at my door any day soon. In fact, I was so convinced that all the good men were either spoken for or sitting at home reading, that the only way I would ever meet one was to go door-to-door selling books!

So, what was the problem? I was nice looking enough, intelligent and fun to be around . . . a great catch for any guy, I thought. Why didn't I have a man?

And then it hit me, my epiphany . . . *I didn't have a man in my life because I wasn't meeting any*!

Duh!

Okay, I may have been a little slow, but it finally occurred to me, if I met more guys, my chances of finding a potential mate would greatly increase as well.

Am I right? If you knew where single men spend their leisure time, what activities they are involved in, and more importantly, what you could do to meet them, wouldn't that increase your chances of finding someone special?

I think so.

And it is this realization that led me to write *Where are the Men?* and share the many ways I have discovered of meeting eligible fellows. It took more than ten years, spending untold hours testing out my ideas, exploring every imaginable possibility in my search of the elusive single male. I attended a myriad of business seminars and luncheons, sat through dozens of classes, consumed too many hot dogs watching Little League games, spent countless hours jogging around parks, and numerous afternoons wandering through hardware and sporting goods stores.

Some things I tried were a complete waste of time. I remember one unproductive evening that was advertised as a way to meet other singles during organized "getting-to-know-you" exercises, and led by two well-known psychologists. Great idea, but where were the men? Of the several hundred attendees . . . almost all were female! (It didn't take long to discover that most activities geared toward personal development and relationships were attended primarily by women.)

On the other hand, many things I tried turned out great. The most successful were those activities dominated by men, so I concentrated my search to opportunities where males were prevalent. One of the most memorable was a woodworking class, where I was the only girl among several dozen guys. Not only did I learn something useful, I had a blast. And did I mention . . . I met a lot of men!

WHERE DO I LOOK?

If I were to ask where you would most likely find single guys, most of you would probably answer, "a singles bar." Sadly, many women (and men for that matter) think this is where the majority of single people meet. Why else are these places packed on Friday evenings? Granted there are a lot of unattached people enjoying the ambiance, but it is not for everyone. At some point you come to the realization there must be other ways of meeting nice guys. (Besides, do you know anyone who has met their Prince Charming in a bar? I rest my case.)

The problem is most of you do not know where else to go. Consequently, many of you have been dateless for some time and have become discouraged about finding someone special. And still others have given up because you think the older you become, the harder it is to find a loving partner. Is it any wonder, then, so many of you are resigned to thinking there are no men out there and are destined to spending the rest of your life alone?

But it doesn't have to be that way. I believe each of you has the ability to meet eligible males and enjoy the benefits of having a man in your life. The only thing holding you back is not knowing where to look.

As every good fisherman knows, you can spend all day looking for fish, but if you're not looking in the right places, you're never going to find them. The same is true if you want to meet single guys, you have to know where they are and place yourself in a position to be there, too.

You won't meet men if you're not where they are!

Unfortunately, too many women have yet to figure out this means participating in activities which males have an interest, particularly those where guys outnumber the gals. Instead most females spend their time doing things where male participation is limited. To show you what I mean, let's take a quiz:

Which of the following activities would you prefer doing:

(1) Attend a seminar on perennials or lawn care?
(2) Learn how to wallpaper or install hardwood floors?
(3) Stitch a needlepoint pillow or build a cabinet?
(4) Have friends over for dinner or play poker?
(5) Take piano lessons or strum a guitar?
(6) Wander through an arts and crafts exhibit or vintage auto show?
(7) Spend the weekend at a spa or a rustic hunting lodge?
(8) Watch an old movie or *Monday Night Football*?

Now go back through the list, which do you think men would choose? Do you see what I'm getting at? Your choices are in direct opposition to what most males would choose. As a general rule, if you find it interesting, men probably will not and vice versa. So what does all this mean? Very simply:

- Either you wait for men to get involved in what interests you . . . in which case *they* will have lots of women to choose from;
- Or you get involved in what interests men . . . in which case *you* will have lots of fellows to choose from.

Here is a partial list of the most common places to find the opposite sex and where we'll concentrate our search:

Where they work . . .
Downtown business districts
Manufacturing and industrial areas
Military bases
Fire/police departments
Construction sites
High-technology companies
Engineering firms

Where they live . . .
Apartment and condominium complexes
Near commercial and business districts
Resorts and other recreational areas
High-tech corridors

What they do in their leisure . . .
Anything having to do with automobiles
Sailing and other water sports
Hobbies
Playing computer and board games
Gambling

Where they recreate . . .
Parks and recreation areas
Jogging paths
Athletic and fitness clubs
Golf courses
Fishing and hunting areas

What they attend . . .
Sporting events
Business affairs and trade shows
Night classes

Public meetings
Fund raisers
Political events

Places they frequent . . .

Sports bars and brew pubs
Happy hours
Cafés for breakfast
Sandwich shops
Truck stops

Groups they join . . .

Sports and recreational groups
Car clubs
Business and computer associations
Private clubs and fraternal organizations
Service groups

Where they shop . . .

Computer, electronic and high-tech suppliers
Music stores
Hardware and building supplies
Hobby shops
Sporting goods and outdoor retailers
Automotive-related stores
Wine and tobacco merchants
Men's clothing and haberdasheries

Where they travel . . .

Hotels near business districts
Golf and ski resorts
Boating and other water-oriented locations
Hunting and outdoor lodges
Gambling destinations

Now that you have some idea of where eligible men can be found, let's proceed with how we're going to meet these fine fellows!

Success Is In The "POP!"

The first step is to develop new attitudes in the way you think and how you approach your life. Don't worry, I'm not going to bore you with a lot of psychological theories or jargon, but I do think it important to discuss what I consider the three main ingredients for meeting our male counterparts and what I have come to call the "POP" principle:

Participate
Be **O**utgoing
Persevere

In order to have success with the opposite sex you must know what opportunities are available to you, which activities men are prevalent and how to position yourself to meet them. Once you are doing things, you then have to get their attention by being friendly and outgoing. And finally, you must be persistent, you cannot give up, as you pursue your goal of finding someone special. Simply put:

Do things
Talk to people
Keep doing it!

Now let's look at each of the elements that make up the *POP*.

2

PARTICIPATE

I wonder if Oprah Winfrey realized when she said, "Luck is a matter of preparation meeting opportunity," that she was also talking about what it takes to find men . . . knowing where they are (preparation) and being in a position to meet them (opportunity).

And how do you discover these prospects? By doing your homework. The amount of time you spend discovering what is out there is proportionate to the number of opportunities for meeting single guys. And every occasion you have to be around the opposite sex increases your chances of encountering someone special. It is so important, let me say it again: *the more opportunities for being around men, the greater your chances of meeting someone new.* And, as with most worthwhile undertakings, a certain amount of preparation is required.

WHAT'S GOING ON?

Begin your search by finding out which activities are available in your locale, paying particular attention to those events that are of interest to men. Anything within a half-hour or more of your home or office should be considered. (You can always reserve weekends for events that are farther away.)

As you compile this information, you may find it helpful to use a date book or computer database to keep track of these possibilities. You will be amazed at the options available to you. As an example, during one week in October, I looked through several publications in the Seattle area and discovered *more than 150 prospects*, ranging from seminars and sporting events to business luncheons, public meetings and special interest functions . . . and all within 30 minutes of my home!

The following suggestions will help you discover what is going on and where you will most likely find eligible men:

TIPS . . .

- **Read newspapers and business publications . . .** including those from neighboring cities and peruse daily for upcoming activities:

    Browse through the business section – look for seminars, meetings and conventions.

    Glance over the sports page – notice college and high school events. Even if you are not a sports enthusiast, be aware of what is going on locally.

    Pay attention to advertisements – particularly in the sports and business sections, which are usually geared toward men.

    Look for special events – check the "Calendar" section for exhibits, auctions and other goings on that men would likely attend.

- **Look through the *Yellow Pages*™.** Discover groups in your locale that you may not be aware of. Check headings, such as *Business and Trade Associations, Clubs* and *Organizations*.

- **Inquire about classes and activities offered . . .** at colleges, libraries, bookstores, home improvement centers, city parks and recreation departments. Also, check with the Small Business Administration and other federal or state agencies.

- **Find out when civic groups meet . . .** city or county councils, arts or planning commissions and other public forums.

- **Put your name on mailing lists.** Stay informed of upcoming events, particularly art galleries, business and charitable groups, clubs and retail outlets.

- **Be aware of special interest organizations.** Contact related stores for information on local clubs and activities.

- **Contact hotels with business facilities.** Talk with banquet personnel to learn when meetings and conferences are scheduled. Check lobby display boards for daily functions.

- **Call nearby churches and synagogues . . .** for church sponsored singles groups and activities.

- **Check references at your public library.** There are many resources for locating specialty organizations, publications and industry related events.

- **Contact Chambers of Commerce . . .** not only are C of Cs a great source of information on local businesses and community affairs, but they also offer numerous functions for members and nonmembers.

- **Find out about upcoming events sponsored by retail merchants.** For example, many sporting goods stores have outdoor excursions and computer outlets offer software classes.

- **Communicate with friends or colleagues in nearby areas.** Ask them to send you news on activities in their vicinity.

- **Be aware of unique opportunities in your locale . . .** such as racetracks, outdoor adventures, or other amusements that males have an interest.

- **Contact your state tourism office . . .** for free travel guides, brochures and event schedules, which they will send to you free of charge.

- **Research the Internet.** There is a wealth of data online for singles on every interest imaginable, including groups and activities that have local connections. In fact, had the Net been available twenty years ago, it would have made my search a whole lot easier!

BE OBSERVANT

We oftentimes fail to "see" what is directly in front of us. It's easy to do. Let's say, for instance, you want to lose a few pounds and tape an unflattering picture of yourself on the refrigerator. (This is so you will look at it every time you open the door.) But what happens several days later when you reach in the freezer for an ice cream? The photo goes unnoticed!

The same is true as we get caught up in our day-to-day activities. Too many of us have become so involved with self, family and careers that we overlook many obvious possibilities. For example, as you drive past the park on Wednesday evening, a group of fellows are playing softball. What do you do? Most likely, you continue on by in your rush to get home.

Hel-loooooooo!

We're talking *several dozen men in one place!* The smart woman will stop the car, walk over to the ballfield and watch them play. And with any kind of luck, she will talk with several of them. (If not this time, maybe next Wednesday when she stops by again.) One thing you will quickly learn is single men tend to hang out with other single males. So when you find a couple of fellows, you'll find a bunch . . . *no one knows more single men than a single man!*

You should be *constantly* looking for opportunities. Be observant and absorb everything around you, especially during commutes and places you frequent. Make note of the day, time and location where you see potential and add to your prospect database. Get to know where popular pedestrian walkways are located, where males are participating in leisure activities and which recreation areas are busiest. Check out parking lots . . . are there many cars, especially ones men often drive, like pickup trucks, four-wheel drives and sports cars? Do any of the trucks have a dog in the back? If so, chances are very good there's a fellow nearby.

FIND OPPORTUNITIES

Think of yourself as a super sleuth. Your ability to locate the opposite sex and seek out those activities where males are abundant is directly related to your potential for meeting unattached gentlemen. And this is where I can help you. Throughout the following chapters you will find hundreds of suggestions for being around men with the main focus on activities where male participation is predominant. Any opportunity you have to be involved in these activities will usually find you outnumbered by the opposite sex. Once you know where to find men, the only effort required on your part is to position yourself to meet them.

3

BE OUTGOING

Why is it that some women seem to attract men without any effort? What is it about these individuals that makes them so successful? Contrary to what you may believe, it is not always good looks. Most females who attract the opposite sex are outgoing, likeable women and enjoy being around people. They are self-assured and do not worry about whether or not a man will like them.

It seems fairly obvious, then, the more you can emulate these ladies, the more attractive you become and the better your chances of meeting someone new. Over the years I have observed four common traits among these magnetic women:

- They are outgoing and quick to smile.
- They initiate conversations.
- They have many interests and are socially active.
- They have a lot of self-confidence.

I have one friend (we'll call her Karen) who is a male magnet. She is friendly, confident and knows how to get a man's attention, as the following story illustrates:

One evening several of us met at a favorite neighborhood bistro for dinner. As usual there was a long wait, so we found a table in the lounge. After sitting down, I leaned over and asked Karen, who was visiting from Texas, what she thought about our little beach town.

"This is great!" she said enthusiastically, "I love places like this . . . and the men are *so* cute. In fact, I've got my eye on one of them over at the bar. I think I'll head over there and order a drink."

Southern women have such an advantage, I thought, remembering my days in Houston. They're such flirts. They think nothing of walking up to some fellow and talking to him. It seems so easy for them . . .

My train of thought was interrupted as Karen returned grinning from ear to ear. "I've just met the cutest guys! Is it okay if they join us?" As we nodded our approval, she motioned toward the bar and within seconds, half a dozen nice looking fellows were sitting at our table. As she began introducing each of them to us, we stared at each other in stunned disbelief. This was amazing! She had not been gone for more than ten minutes . . . what could she possibly have done to attract so many men?

I had to know her secret and later that night asked how she did it. She looked at me questioningly and answered in her southern drawl: *I didn't do anything special. When I went to the bar and ordered my drink, I just squeezed between a couple of guys, smiled and said, "Hi, y'all!"*

My friend may never know what she has done for single women, but what she taught me that night was a turning point for me and became my credo for meeting men:

- Purchase your drinks from the bar.
- Place yourself between several guys.
- Look them in the eyes, smile and say, "Hi, y'all!"

In all seriousness, what actually happened that night? First, my friend noticed where the men were (at the bar) and placed herself in the middle of them (ordering her drink). Secondly, she initiated the conversation and invited them to join us.

So there it is, the two most important criteria for meeting men: *be where they are* and *talk to them!*

TALK TO THEM

If you want to meet men, you have to talk to them. It's as simple as that. It doesn't cost a thing to be friendly and outgoing, to smile at someone, or ask how their day is going. Make it a habit to talk to people. Be the first to offer a warm smile or friendly greeting. Turn around and chat with the person in line behind you or the guy sitting next to you. It's easy to do and could lead to a wonderful new friendship.

Initiate a conversation, comment about what the two of you are looking at or participating in. Find a reason to be in contact again. Is there some information you can share like an article you've read, a recipe you've tried, or a group you know about?

Carry several business cards for these occasions or offer a personal card with a description of yourself, such as "Mary Smith, Seattle's best kept secret," "Carol Adams, mystery writer," or "June Brown, fun-loving Grandmother."

Show genuine enthusiasm when talking to people, maintain eye contact as you share good news, like something you've done or are anticipating. If you show an interest with whom you are talking and bring a warm and pleasing personality to all your encounters, people will want to be around you.

Obviously, there will be times when things just are not going the way you want them. That's understandable, but do not bring those "harumph" days with you when out looking for men. No one enjoys being around someone who is negative or unhappy. Keep in mind, you are striving to become a male magnet . . . you want to attract men, not repel them.

I learned this valuable lesson one evening when I bumped into a fellow I had been admiring. I was still frothing about something that had happened earlier at the office and when he asked, "How are you?" I unloaded my pent up frustrations and told him *exactly* how bad my day had gone. Within minutes he was making excuses as to why he couldn't stay and talk longer. But that's not the end of the story, every time I saw him after that, he was always in a hurry to get somewhere else. Remember, first impressions only happen once, so stay upbeat and positive.

And don't limit yourself only to men. *Every* person you meet opens the possibility of meeting their fathers, brothers, uncles, sons, grandfathers, friends, neighbors and colleagues who may be single. You just never know where a casual conversation may lead . . . I met a wonderful man through a blind date that resulted after talking with a woman while waiting in the doctor's office!

Here are a few ideas to help you interact with people:

TIPS . . .

- **Ask for directions or suggestions.** "If you were (thirsty, hungry, having a bad hair day) right now, where would you go?" "Where's the nearest (ice cream parlor, espresso stand)?" "Where can I find . . .?"
- **Start a conversation using humorous one-liners.** Try one of these: "Are we having fun yet?" "Were you put in charge of this weather today?" "I know if we wait here long enough something will happen." "How's your day going on a scale of one to ten?"
- **Talk to someone in the elevator.** Comment on how a local sports team is doing, the weather, or why no one ever talks in the elevator.
- **Introduce yourself to a stranger.** A neighbor you haven't met, the person sitting next to you, someone who works or lives in the same building.
- **Do things on your own.** You will discover men are more willing to approach you when you are by yourself and

you are more likely to initiate conversations with individuals when you are alone.

- **Lighten up and have fun.** Think of the people you like being around. Aren't they enjoyable? Don't they make you laugh and feel good?
- **Do not use drive-thrus.** You are not going to meet men sitting in your automobile. Always get out of the car and go inside. This includes fast food places and banks.
- **Think of waiting in line as an opportunity . . .** the longer the wait, the more time you have to talk to that fellow behind you.
- **Always look your best.** Be prepared to meet someone special every time you leave the house.

CULTIVATE FRIENDSHIPS

The following old Chinese proverb is a great analogy for what can happen when you begin meeting people and cultivating friendships. The story begins with a King in great peril . . . an elderly peasant who happens by, rescues the King from certain death and wanting to thank the old man, the King asks what he can offer him in return:

Knowing the King to be a greedy and stingy ruler, the peasant replied, "All I ask is for you to place a grain of rice on the first square of a chess board, on the next square place two grains of rice and continue to double the amount until each square is filled."

"Is that all you want?" the King asked, "that seems like such a small request," and he summoned his staff to begin placing the grain on the board. As the King watched, he was astonished to see how large the piles of rice were becoming and by the time his helpers had finished, not one grain of rice was left in all his kingdom.

The moral to the story: great rewards can come from very small beginnings.

Each person you meet represents an exponential growth in friendships. Let's say you meet John and he has two unattached friends he introduces you to. Each of them has two friends, who introduces you to two of their friends and so on. By the time you meet the friends of the friends of John's friends (whew!), you will have met 31 people!

CAN YOU BELIEVE HE TALKED TO ME?

Are you uncomfortable talking to strangers? Do you worry about what to say or how you will feel if someone doesn't respond positively? Maybe you're not the type of person who can walk up to someone and start talking to them, but let's be frank, if you want to start meeting men, you must overcome this fear.

The more you talk to people, the easier it becomes, and the easier it becomes, the more confident you are. One begets the other, until one day you don't worry about it any more. If you don't believe me, try smiling at that handsome man in the elevator and then ask what he thinks about the beautiful day outside. This may surprise you, but he *will* answer you back. Then the next time you see him you will be more comfortable talking to him and it continues to get easier each time thereafter.

And besides, what's the worst thing that can happen? He ignores you or gives you a negative response? Clearly, no one enjoys being rejected, but you must not take it personally if someone does not return your friendliness. It happens. There could be a number of reasons why he doesn't want to talk with you right now . . . he doesn't feel well or had a bad day at the office. The important thing is not to dwell on it or worse, let it affect your self-esteem. Focus on the positive, feel good about yourself and what you have to offer. Remember, he is the one who has lost out.

But there is another possibility. What if it turns out, he has wanted to talk to you, too. Believe it or not, many men are just as timid as you.

One male acquaintance confided in me that he had been admiring a woman he jogged past in the mornings, but was afraid to talk to her. When I asked why, he said he didn't know what to say to her and besides he thought for sure she was spoken for. I suggested the next time he see her, he strike up a casual conversation saying something friendly, like "How far are you running?" and if she didn't feel like talking to him, he could continue on with his run.

The next time I saw him, I asked how his conversation had gone. "I still can't believe it! We hit it off so well," he said. "In fact, we've had several dates and are enjoying each other tremendously!"

Apparently she, too, had been admiring him and all it took was one of them saying something.

I think whoever said, "Nothing ventured, nothing gained" had it right. Several years ago one friend of mine who "had nothing to lose," met a well-known recording artist this way. One morning on her hour-plus commute, a late-model automobile passed her. Noticing the solitary male behind the wheel, she sped up, keeping pace with him, until he realized she was trying to get his attention. Being the confident, outgoing person that she is, when he looked over, she smiled and waved. After several miles of this, he motioned for her to follow him to the next exit. As it turned out, he was on his way to a recording session, enjoyed her flirtation and wanted to meet her over a cup of coffee.

Although this chance meeting did not have a fairy tale ending, my friend would never have had the opportunity to meet this handsome celebrity had she not taken the initiative. Clearly, not everyone has the courage to put herself out there and risk the possibility of rejection, but if you don't do it, how will you ever know otherwise?

UNCOMFORTABLE SITUATIONS

What do you do when you don't know anyone? I remember the first time this happened to me at a Chamber of Commerce function. I walked in and everyone was in small groups. I froze. I don't know what I expected, but I was so frightened I immediately turned around and spent the next fifteen minutes in the restroom waiting for the meeting to begin.

Even though I have faced many similar situations since then, I am happy to say it's no longer quite so frightening. So what should you do? In circumstances like this, you have several options:

- Go to the restroom and wait until everyone in the other room is seated . . . as I did.
- Turn around and leave . . . and tell yourself you probably didn't need to be there anyway.
- Stand off by yourself and hope someone approaches you.
- Take a seat and wait for the event to begin.
- Walk up to someone and start a conversation.
- Approach a group and listen to their discussion.

I suggest the latter two. Walk up to the group and say, "Hi, I'm by myself and don't know anyone. Can I listen in on what you're talking about?" Or walk up to someone, extend your hand and say, "Hi, I'm Susan, what do you think about what we're going to hear?" There is virtually no one who will tell you to go away.

And while we are on the subject, one of my pet peeves is a woman who thinks extending a limp hand is equivalent to a handshake. If you are going to shake someone's hand, then do so. Grab hold of the man's right hand and give it a gentle, but firm squeeze. You will find that not only do men place more importance on this gesture than you realize, but a good handshake will also show you have self-confidence.

APPROACHING A GROUP

If you have a choice of approaching a group of men or women, go for the guys! You may think you will be more comfortable with the gals, but don't do it. First off, there are no males to meet in a group of women and secondly, the men will be more open to you. And better yet, while the other women are talking amongst themselves, you will be conversing with several interesting gentlemen!

At a recent luncheon I arrived late and luckily for me most of the attendees were already seated at their tables. (Not that I make it a practice of arriving late, but it does afford the opportunity of seeing where everyone is seated.) As I scanned the room, I noticed several empty seats – one was at a table of ladies, several were at tables with both men and women, and one empty seat was at a table of men. Guess where I went?

By the time the luncheon was over, not only did I have the delight of being the only woman with seven men, I also made contact with a future banker and a venture capitalist. You will discover that most people are very cordial in business environments. They are there to make contact with other business people and are very interested in what you do and what you may have to offer them, and vice versa.

By the way, what do you think most of the other women in the room were doing? That's right. They were talking to other women. No wonder so many of you never meet any men.

4

PERSEVERE

Perseverance is defined in the World Book Encyclopedia Dictionary as: *Holding fast to a purpose or course of action . . . refusing to be discouraged by obstacles or difficulties, but continuing steadily with courage and patience: Perseverance leads to success.* In other words, perseverance is the determination, the staying power you must have to find eligible men. It is wanting something so much that you exhaust every possibility before going on to something else.

For example, if you were to go on a diet for two weeks, and at the end of that time you hadn't lost an ounce, you wouldn't have much incentive to stick with the diet, would you? But if your desire is strong enough to lose weight, you would most likely re-evaluate what you had been doing . . . are you eating too many chips, using too much butter, or not getting enough exercise. And if you are honest with yourself, you will see where you've gone astray, make the necessary adjustments and stick with it until you get the desired results. This same tenacity and desire are necessary to find a man. Remember . . . *perseverance leads to success*, it does not lead to failure.

Obviously things will not always turn out the way you planned, but if you stay focused and concentrate on your objective of participating in activities where men are in the majority, it won't be long before you find someone special. Now don't misunderstand, this does not mean that finding a man will be easy or that every guy you meet will be "the one." Remember the old saying, "you have to kiss a few toads . . ." It takes time and effort to find a potential mate, but you *will* find happiness and someone to love if you stick with it. I know it is possible. It took me ten years and a lot of toads . . . but I eventually found my Prince Charming.

FIND THE TIME

Get out whenever you can, go places and get involved in a variety of things. If you don't want to participate in a particular activity, be a spectator instead. For instance, if you're not into running, then situate yourself near the jogging path so you can still speak to individuals as they run past. Remember, the more you place yourself in public places and around people, the greater your chances of meeting someone new.

And finally, if time is an issue, instead of thinking in days or hours, think in minutes. There are 1,440 minutes in a day, 480 may be spent working, 420 sleeping and 45 commuting. See what you can do with the remaining 495 minutes.

KEEP AT IT

During my quest for men, one of my "pick-up-everything-I-own-and-put-it-in-the-back-of-a-U-Haul" relocations was to Houston, Texas. One of six moves in a span of three years – no, I wasn't crazy, I just enjoyed moving to new places and seeing how well the *POP* theory worked. After getting to know the area, I decided a good place to meet single men was at Memorial Park, a popular jogging area. So each evening after work I put on my tennis shoes and shorts and walked along the running path. (Jogging was out of the question, as I could barely make it up a flight of stairs before collapsing!)

At first I felt out-of-place, as I seemed to be the only one who was not jogging. But I didn't let that discourage me as I continued with my walks, night after night, week after week, until I began noticing familiar faces and would smile and acknowledge them with a friendly "Hi!" as they ran past. One evening, a fellow I'd been smiling at, came alongside me and said, "Come on now, you've walked enough."

"But I'm not a jogger," I whined.

"Oh, come on, I know you can do it. Just run with me as far as that white pole up there." And with that he grabbed my elbow and off we went. Although I pooped out before getting to the pole, it did not discourage him from urging me to run a little farther each time he saw me after that. And before I realized it, not only was I actually jogging, I had a new friend!

Over the next several months, I continued to meet more runners and cultivated several new friendships that not only kept my phone ringing, but my Friday and Saturday nights filled. And all because of persistence . . . both by my discipline in going there every evening and my determination (and my friend's urging) to run just a little farther each day. (And on a proud note, the following year I ran my first marathon, all 26.2 miles of it!)

Every time you leave the house presents an opportunity to meet someone . . . jogging around your neighborhood, sitting on a park bench, or riding the bus. And the more often you do it, the better your chances of seeing a familiar face. This means frequenting the same places and being friendly, and before you know it, you will be talking to people and making new friends.

Let's see how this works. Suppose you try one of my suggestions and get a cappuccino at a coffeehouse on your way to work. Most mornings you see a guy by himself, sometimes he's reading the paper, other times he's talking with other customers. This is your target. The next couple of times you see him you exchange pleasantries until you are comfortably talking with each other and then one day he asks you to join him.

But what if he's not interested? No problem, just find another target, and if there are no other prospects, try a different time of day or go somewhere else. Keep doing this until you have exhausted all possibilities before going on to some other activity.

MOTIVATION . . . IT'S UP TO YOU!

But what if things move too slowly and you get discouraged? How do you persevere if you give up too easily?

The answer is to believe in yourself and know that what you truly desire will come to you. Did you get that? The secret is not to *think* you *might*, but *know* you *will* get what you truly desire. Big difference. This should be foremost in your thinking and activity planning.

Start each day with optimism, look forward to good things happening to you, especially when you're not seeing immediate results or your first few efforts end in disappointment. Continue to tell yourself that happiness is waiting for you and it's just around the corner. Think of it as a good book, every day is a new page . . . and today's page has its corner turned down!

Unfortunately, too many women fail to recognize how important motivation really is. The worst thing you can do is make excuses for lack of initiative – I'm too tired, I don't have the time, I'm not ready yet, I'm too old. Unfortunately, none of these excuses are going to get you out with people or find you a man.

Some years ago, a close friend of mine found herself in one of these motivational pits. She had become so comfortable in her little apartment with her two cats that she hardly ever ventured out. It takes some effort to put yourself out there, to risk rejection, but rather than take a chance on having a negative response, some of you become content to stay in your own little secure worlds. There is a reason some women are successful and why some are not.

My dear friend, Mitzi, met more men than anyone I've ever known. In her late seventies, she was a loveable, offbeat woman, much like the character Ruth Gordon played in *Harold and Maude*. One day after telling me about the latest fellow she'd met, I asked how she was able to find so many. She grinned impishly as she told me how she would go to the shopping mall around the dinner hour and wait outside one of the restaurants until a man walked in and sat at the counter. Then she would go in, sit next to him, smile and say something cute, like, "Hi, it looks as if we'll be dining together. My name's Mitzi, what's yours?" She did this several times a week and met many interesting men, both young and old.

You and you alone are responsible for the choices you make, the extent of your involvement and commitment to meeting people and making friends. There is no one else who can do it for you. It's up to you to get out of the house, to go places and do things that will put you around people. Think of it as an investment, the more you put into it, the more you will get back.

5

It's Your Choice

If you've been paying any attention, by now you should have some idea of how you're going to find men. But before getting into specifics, let's look at the choices you make in your day-to-day activities.

There is no denying that we are creatures of habit. We do the same things day after day . . . we go through the same morning routine before work, we eat in the lunchroom with the same co-workers and we lounge around the house most Saturday mornings. We also make decisions as to how we'll carry out these activities . . . whether to do our morning stretching exercises or not; whether to bring our lunch or not; whether to sleep in or not.

But there are other ways to accomplish these activities that will allow more opportunities for meeting men. It's just a matter of thinking about how you go about your day and considering other alternatives. As an example, let's look at two different women getting ready for work:

> Carol gets up at 6:30, showers, has a glass of juice and toast before heading out the door and driving to work. After

arriving at her office, she gets a cup of coffee from the lunchroom, talks to a co-worker and is sitting at her desk by 8:00.

Sally gets up at 6:00, jogs around her neighborhood and exchanges pleasantries with several runners. After showering, she takes the bus to work and talks to the man sitting next to her about the product he sells. She then stops by a coffee bar next to her building for an espresso and croissant and chats with a male customer who looks familiar. And by 8:00 she, too, is sitting at her desk.

Whom do you think has the best chance of meeting someone new? In the first scenario, Carol spends $1^1/_2$ hours and comes in contact with one person, her co-worker. But Sally, on the other hand, spends 2 hours and comes in contact with several new people.

TRY SOMETHING DIFFERENT

Think about your daily routine, what can you do differently that will put you around people? Instead of eating in the lunchroom, why not go to a nearby restaurant and talk to the fellow sitting next to you. Or rather than sleeping in on the weekend, get up early and go for a walk, then stop for a cappuccino at an outdoor café and visit with other morning people.

Here are a few alternatives to your normal routine that you may want to consider:

Instead of getting ready for work as usual, get up an hour earlier . . .
Go for a run or a walk and meet other early risers.
Or work out at the gym.

◆

Instead of having breakfast at home . . .
Eat at a local café.

Grab a cinnamon roll at an espresso bar.
Or network with other business people at a breakfast meeting.

✦

Instead of reading the morning paper at home . . .
Peruse the sports pages at a coffeehouse.
Look through the financials in the lobby of an office building.
Or read it while you are on the bus.

✦

Instead of driving to work . . .
Participate in a carpool.
Or use public transportation.

✦

Instead of lunch at your desk . . .
Get outside during the noon hour.
Attend a business luncheon.
Run a few errands.
Or try one of the "During the Lunch Hour" ideas on pages 61-63.

✦

Instead of going directly home after work . . .
Walk or jog around the park.
Attend a civic meeting.
Hit a bucket of balls.
Or take a night class.

✦

Instead of eating dinner at home . . .
Have a light supper at a local café.
Or attempt one of the "Dining Alone" suggestions on pages 155-159.

✦

Instead of sleeping in on the weekend . . .
Go out for breakfast.
Take a class in computer programming.
Or volunteer to do something.

✦

Instead of reading at home . . .
Read on a bench near a busy promenade.
Curl up with a magazine in the lobby of a hotel.
Or find an interesting book and read it at the library or
   bookstore.

✦

Instead of watching television in the evening . . .
Go to a Little League game at a nearby park.
Take an after dinner walk.
Or give any "After Hours" ideas on pages 160-163 a try.

✦

Instead of spending the weekend at home . . .
Pick out one of the "Weekend Getaways" suggestions on
   pages 145-146.

✦

Instead of taking a "female-type" class . . .
Take golf lessons.
Attend a "how-to" at a home center.
Or try any of the "Learn Something New" activities on
   pages 97-98.

✦

Instead of shopping at a department store . . .
Get fitted for hiking boots at a sporting goods outlet.
Try on bluejeans at a men's store.
Look for a small appliance at a hardware emporium.
Or seek out other alternatives, such as in Chapter 10,
   WHERE THEY SHOP.

✦

Instead of washing clothes at home . . .
Go to a laundromat with a bar or restaurant next door.
Or find a coin-operated place near an apartment complex.

✦ ✦ ✦

It's *your* choice, it's up to you to seriously consider the decisions
you make. It takes very little effort to try something else and be
around men.

BE OPEN TO ALL OPPORTUNITIES

Do not limit yourself only to activities which you have some knowledge or expertise. Many of us do the same things with the same people and lack the imagination to try new things. There are hundreds of opportunities out there where men are the major participants which you may not be aware of – some of these you will want to pursue, others you may prefer leaving alone.

Even if you do not have any interest in a popular male activity, try to find something associated with it that you might enjoy. Let's take golf as an example. There are many opportunities to meet golfers without having to pick up a golf club . . . you can visit a golf course and have lunch, look for a cute shirt in the pro shop, or join a country club and partake in the social activities. The important thing to remember is just because you have no desire to be a part of a particular activity, do not rule out anyone involved in it.

Unfortunately, many women think it is a waste of time to cultivate relationships with men whom they cannot relate. I recently suggested to a colleague of mine she take up golf to meet single fellows. "I'm not a physical person," she replied, "and quite frankly I don't want to waste my time with someone who is not going to spend time with me." On the surface this may seem acceptable, but if we take this one step further, let's see what she has actually done by eliminating all golfers and related activities.

According to the National Golf Foundation there are nearly 19 million adult male golfers in North America. If we assume 25% are single, this means she has eliminated almost five million eligible men from her search. Add this to all the other sports and activities she may not have an interest, and guess what? Her odds of finding a man become greater than winning the lottery!

And while we're on the subject, let me clear up a few preconceived notions that many women have about men who play golf. The majority of golf enthusiasts do not spend every waking moment pursuing their sport. In fact, most men think of themselves as well-rounded fellows and participate in a variety of activities including golf.

And, being married to a golfer isn't so bad. One of my closest friend's husbands is an avid golfer. Even though she wishes he would spend more time with her instead of his golfing buddies, she uses this time to get together with her lady friends and pursue other interests, like canning and quilting, which he is not included.

Besides, I think if most women had their choice of living alone or being with an avid golfer who loves them dearly, they'd take the golfer every time!

This may seem harsh, but if you are willing to rule out millions of single men because they enjoy doing some sport that you do not, I am afraid you are destined to sitting at home and growing old alone. It is very rare to find a man who is not actively involved in or does not enjoy watching some sports activity.

The point is you are not going to settle down with every man you encounter. Clearly if you have champagne and haute cuisine tastes you may not be comfortable with a chili and beer guy. But all you are trying to do at this point is meet people, especially the male species, and if you are too selective with the men you do encounter, you may miss out on meeting one of their buddies or co-workers who may be more suited to you.

6

Final Thoughts

Okay, you're almost ready to get out there and start meeting some fellows. But before you do, there are a few other areas I'd like to touch on that I believe are relevant to finding unattached men.

Affirmations and Visualization

Affirmations and visualization are two popular techniques for instructing your subconscious mind to guide you to your desired goal. I don't know how it all works, but it's just like driving an automobile: you don't need to know how petroleum is introduced into a cylinder and ignites, causing an explosion that forces the piston down, turning the shaft which spins the wheels. All you need to know: push on the gas pedal and the car moves.

Some years ago I attended a self-hypnosis seminar hoping to improve my visualization skills. The psychologist, leading our group, told us about a client who wanted to lose weight. She suggested the client use visualization and see herself as some object getting smaller.

A few weeks later her client called and was quite distressed, "I don't know what's going on, but I have a horrible perspiration problem and have been sweating profusely! What am I doing wrong?"

The psychologist asked what she had been visualizing and she answered, "a melting ice cube."

Be careful what you visualize. Your subconscious does exactly what it is instructed to do. It is not able to reason or figure out what you may mean.

Affirmations are like visualization. The process involves writing down exactly what you want and reading this aloud several times a day. According to Napoleon Hill in his best-selling book, *Think and Grow Rich*, "Through repetition of this procedure, you voluntarily create thought habits which are favorable to your efforts to transmute desire . . ." to ultimately reach the hoped for result. In other words, if you want it bad enough, it will happen!

When I first decided to take matters into my own hands and find a man, the first thing I did was make up my wish list . . . *I want the man in my life to be tall, have a good sense of humor, be sensitive and romantic, love the out-of-doors, dogs, dancing* and so on. Every night before going to sleep and every morning upon awakening, not only did I read aloud my affirmations, but I also visualized myself in the arms of this tall, wonderfully romantic, sensitive man.

I believe in affirmations and visualization . . . it worked for me and it can work for you. Trust me here. Even if you have doubts, do it anyway. There is no harm done, and if you find it works, write and thank me for insisting that you try it.

HOW DO I KNOW HE'S NOT A WACKO?

Unfortunately, this is a major concern for many women. My best advice is to listen to your inner feelings. If you are the least bit uncomfortable, don't let it go any further – and tell him you are not interested. But do not give him your home phone number, address, or any personal information during your first encounter. Give him your first name only, especially if you are listed in the phone book.

If you consider seeing him again, meet on common ground in a non-threatening situation . . . such as breakfast or lunch near his office (so you can see where he works). Have a couple of your friends and a couple of his pals join the two of you for dinner. If he's new in town and has yet to make any friends, ask him to invite one or two of his co-workers. What you are trying to discover is how others act toward him and whether or not he is well-liked by those he associates with.

Spend as much time as necessary getting to know him before opening yourself to a possibly bad situation. Generally, the more you know about what he does for a living, what his friends are like, the better off you'll be. Most men will understand your desire to get to know them before you give out any personal information.

I remember when I had my first date with my husband, even though we had spent many hours talking at his office and on the phone, when he picked me up for our date it was at a friend's house. You can never be too careful!

FINDING MONEY

Mitzi, taught me a lot about meeting affluent men. "If you want to attract money, you have to look like you have it," she would say. "You just never know when a wealthy fellow will be standing next to you." She should know . . . of the four men she married, three were millionaires.

Some of you may think those who advocate, "you can fall in love with a rich man just as easily as a poor man" are cold and calculating, but if that is what you desire, then by all means go for it. A recent survey in *Woman's World* magazine revealed 80% of their readership would rather be happy than rich. So I ask you, "Why not happy *and* rich?"

Throughout the following chapters, I've identified specific opportunities where you will most likely meet affluent men. They are marked with a **$**. If a wealthy man is what you are looking for, pay particular attention to these suggestions.

ARE YOU READY?

Now comes the fun part! Throughout *Where are the Men?* you will find hundreds of suggestions to place you around eligible fellows. Not all will appeal to you, so highlight those that do and maybe even some that seem offbeat or adventuresome. And then it's up to you. The important thing is to enjoy yourself and not be concerned with the end result. Remember, all it takes is for one of these to work!

So, let's get going. Get out of the house, start doing things and interacting with people. It won't be long before you find you are happier and enjoying life more. And that's when it will happen, when you least expect it . . . your Knight in Shining Armor will walk up to you, smile and say, "Hi, my name's Mike. What's yours?"

PART 2

OPPORTUNITIES

"Nothing is gained from doing nothing."
— Shakespeare

7

WHERE THEY WORK AND LIVE

The first place to begin looking for available men is where they spend the most amount of time . . . where they work and where they live. In the next few pages are many suggestions to help you locate unattached fellows in both of these environments. Give a few of them a try. . . you'll be happy with the results!

THE WORKPLACE

Statistics indicate that a large number of couples who get married, meet through work. So, it only makes sense to get to know as many of your co-workers as possible. However, this may be difficult to do if you work for a small company, but once you know where to look for eligible men during the workday, you can concentrate your efforts in these areas.

Be aware of which businesses are predominately male and where they are located. Most workers will frequent places near their offices during the workday, so the more often you are in the general vicinity, the greater the probability of meeting someone of interest. Here are a few male-dominated businesses you should check out:

- *High-technology* – such as software and computer related companies
- *Engineering* – civil, electrical and structural firms
- *Construction and manufacturing industries*
- *Legal and financial firms*

✦

Patronize restaurants and retail stores in downtown commercial districts. This is the hub of business activity and the best times to meet businessmen is prior to work, during the lunch hour, or at the end of the day. Again, anytime you can place yourself in the area during these times, will be to your benefit.

✦ ✦ ✦

AT THE OFFICE . . .

Get your first cup of coffee in the morning from an espresso bar. This gives you an opportunity to meet male patrons from nearby offices who regularly stop by before work.

✦

If you use an elevator, wait in the lobby until a gentleman enters . . . then stand next to him and start talking to him. Don't be shy, you can do it!

✦

$ Notice automobiles in reserved stalls . . . and where expensive sports cars are parked. Chances are very good there's a man attached to each one. Wait nearby until one of them arrives and talk with him as you walk to the lobby.

✦

Pay attention to arrival and departure times of men in your building. Many unmarried executives arrive early and stay late, so plan your arrivals and departures accordingly. Then place yourself in the parking lot or near the elevator when they are most likely to be there. After that . . . you know what to do!

✦

During your breaks, get out of the office. Go to a restroom on another floor, stroll down to the lobby and chat with someone, or get out of the building for fifteen minutes and walk around. Any occasion you have to come in contact with other workers or visitors is to your advantage.

✦ ✦ ✦

DURING THE LUNCH HOUR . . .

Go out to lunch as often as possible. The more you dine out, the greater your chances of meeting someone on his lunch hour. If you see a fellow sitting alone, why not join him. It's easy to do particularly during the noon rush when empty tables are at a premium.

✦

Arrive at busy restaurants before they fill up . . . and ask the hostess to seat other solo diners at your table. Not only will you have someone to converse with, but you will meet many interesting people this way.

✦

Notice where male prospects are headed for lunch . . . and go there, too. Individuals who dine out a lot usually patronize two or three favorite places. Make sure you eat there as often as possible.

✦

Frequent a favorite deli for lunch . . . and get to know other repeat customers. The more often you go somewhere, the more you will get to know those who come in on a regular basis . . . and you just never know where a casual encounter may lead!

✦

Visit nearby office buildings during the noon hour . . . and be friendly with other employees who are wandering about. There is no rule that says you have to limit yourself only to those individuals who work in your office.

✦

On a nice day get out where businessmen are milling around. Warm weather brings office workers outside and this is your chance to mingle with them. When brown bagging it, place yourself near busy pedestrian areas, in courtyards, or city parks, and visit with other workers enjoying this time away from the office.

✦

Sit near the entrance of an office building and eat your lunch . . . and acknowledge gentlemen as they come and go. Do this with some frequency and you will become familiar with several of them. But there is one catch . . . if you do this enough, you may end up meeting the man you've been looking for!

✦

Run errands during your noon break . . . particularly those within walking distance of your office. This is when male workers in the vicinity will probably be doing the same.

✦

Bring your lunch to an outdoor concert. Find a spot next to a nice looking gent and see where a little conversation and good music leads.

✦

Eat an early meal at a deli near a construction project. Building crews start work early, so they're hungry earlier, usually between 11 to 11:30. If the sandwiches are piled high and don't cost much, they will be there en masse.

✦

Stop by a sandwich shop near an industrial or manufacturing area . . . where you will find a large number of men. Here again, good, inexpensive sandwich places will be packed with guys during the noon hour. Also, "sub" shops that offer large submarine-style sandwiches are extremely popular with fellows.

✦

If you see a vending truck, stop and get a sandwich. Look for these mobile eateries at construction sites and in parking lots at large office complexes during the mid-morning. You might be surprised with what you can pick up!

✦

Set up a checking account with a bank in an office high-rise. Many men who work in the building will also bank there. Do your deposits and withdrawals during lunch time, especially on Fridays, when businessmen will be doing their banking prior to the weekend.

✦

Attend a luncheon meeting . . . many civic and business groups meet during the noon hour and welcome guests. Besides, can you think of a better way to spend your lunch hour than with a group of handsome executives!

✦ ✦ ✦

OTHER OPTIONS . . .

Visit establishments near military bases. If you're looking for a working environment with a large number of men . . . this is it! There aren't too many other locales with a greater concentration of fellows than these government installations. Since they are off-limits to the general public, the next best thing is to be where they go when they leave the base . . . and then you'll be there to reap the benefits!

✦

Sit in on a trial at the county courthouse. Most civil and criminal courtrooms are open to the public and will make for a very interesting day, not to mention the potential of meeting numerous male witnesses, jury members and barristers who are involved in court proceedings. Be sure to stop by the snack bar first thing in the morning and during recesses . . . it will be a very busy place!

✦

Volunteer to help out at a hospital. If you want to meet doctors, your best bet is to be where they spend the majority of their time. Plus, you'll be there to meet all those men who are visiting the hospital for other reasons. Remember, all it takes is being at the right place at the right time!

✦

Spend time in a public library from 9-5. If it is near a downtown district, the business section will be crowded during the week with men doing industry-related research. Stop by . . . as it definitely is worth checking out!

✦

Use public transportation. If you normally drive to work, leave your car at the park 'n' ride a few days a week. Use this time to make a new friend and chat with your seatmate.

✦

Park your car several blocks away from your office and walk the rest of the way. Change your route periodically so you will be passing by different people each day. If you see an espresso bar, by all means, stop in for a café au lait and see who else is there.

✦

Enroll at a fitness club . . . and exercise routinely at lunch or before and after work. This is a great way to meet lots of businessmen, especially if located near a commercial area. Spend your time in the weight room or on the sports court, where the majority of fellows will be.

✦

Keep your eye on coffeehouses next to retail stores that males frequent . . . such as computer outlets, motorcycle shops and sporting goods stores. Not only will many male patrons stop by after shopping, but workers from nearby businesses will take their breaks there, also.

✦ ✦ ✦

JOB HUNTING . . .

Consider changing your job. To increase your potential of meeting men, look for opportunities with companies that have either a lot of male employees or male clientele. For example, working in a construction company will put you in contact with both building crews and subcontractors.

✦

Seek employment with a temporary agency . . . and work at a different company every week or two. This is a great way to receive a nice income and make many new friendships.

✦

Look for a part-time job that puts you in contact with lots of fellows. Waitressing first comes to mind, especially at breakfast spots and other places males frequent, like fraternal clubs and sports-related establishments. A weekend or couple nights a week could give you a new lease on life!

✦

Learn a trade in a field where men are prevalent . . . such as barbers, who have a constant flow of male customers. Other possibilities include bartending, truck driving, construction and electronics repair. Any new endeavor that will place you around men is ideal.

✦

Get MCSE certified. This is Microsoft's Certified Systems Engineer program and is well worth doing, both in salary potential and the number of men you will come in contact with. First, you will be surrounded by men while taking the required classes. Secondly, once certified you will be in great demand and paid handsomely. And finally, your new position will put you in the technical mainstream where you will be working with even more men. If you have any computer savvy whatsoever, do not hesitate . . . it doesn't get any better than this!

✦ ✦ ✦

WAYS TO MEET CO-WORKERS . . .

If you work for a large company, you probably don't know all your workmates. The quickest way to start meeting other employees is to find a reason to be in contact with them. Here are a few ideas to try:

Publish a company newsletter. This will give you a chance to talk with lots of people, including fellows you don't know very well or haven't yet met. Once you pick out a couple of prospects, interview them for a future news article and in the process find out their interests and what activities they would participate in, if available. Then later, when you are organizing group functions, you'll know what appeals to them and can gear your events accordingly.

✦

Circulate a sports pool. Football is probably the most popular with office workers. If you need help putting one together, ask a male friend to give you a hand. Then during your breaks and lunch hour you can interact with colleagues who want to wager on the games. After several weeks of this you will be well-known to all the fellows!

✦

Buy a new computer action game . . . and challenge someone to beat your score. Many men enjoy playing games and will love showing off their gaming skills. If the software is networkable and it's okay with your LAN administrator, load it on the server and have an office competition during the lunch hour. Later on you can get together for dinner and give recognition to the best gamers.

✦

Ask a male co-worker to join you for lunch. Is there someone you haven't met or who you've had your eye on? This is your chance to get to know him better. Go ahead and do it . . . what have you got to lose!

✦

If you eat in the company cafeteria, sit with someone new tomorrow. When you see a male employee eating alone, ask to join him. Don't be shy, remember . . . nothing ventured, nothing gained.

✦ ✦ ✦

GETTING WORKMATES TOGETHER . . .

Another effective way to meet your colleagues is to put together activities for their participation. Plus, there are added benefits when you are the organizer – not only do you have initial contact with individuals prior to the event, but you will also know everyone who joins in.

To get the word out, print up hand-outs and post notices on bulletin boards, in the cafeteria and restrooms, or include information in the company newsletter. If you do not have an employee base to draw from, distribute flyers to other nearby offices.

Find several fellows for a game of cards during the lunch hour.
Play something fun that most people are familiar with, like Hearts or Pinochle. And don't be surprised if this turns out to be such a hit you will want to continue playing one evening a month, if not more frequently. Be sure to let everyone know any friends they bring along are welcome to play, too.

✦

Get a band or singing group together . . . and perform at company events or around town at shopping malls and parks. The more frequently the group gets together to practice, the closer everyone will become. So the more men that are involved, the more male friendships you'll cultivate.

✦

Form a drill team. Why not get a few employees together to march in an upcoming parade? Many communities celebrate with offbeat cavalcades – you've probably heard of the zany antics of the annual *DooDah Parade* in Pasadena, California. In fact, it's become so popular that many other cities around the country are also featuring offshoots of this nutty celebration. The idea is to be as innovative and crazy as possible – noteworthy entrants from past events are the suitcase and lawn mower drill teams, as well as the SWAT Team, a very funny group of precision fly swatters. Come up with a silly theme . . . such as "the over the hill gang" (where participants wear old folks costumes, carry canes and moan and groan during maneuvers) and use household apparatus for props, like brooms, folding chairs and cordless appliances. Or members can also transport themselves on tricycles, skateboards, or broomstick horses. Just be creative, have fun and meet regularly to work out "intricate" routines. Not only will you have a great time, but I'll bet you will meet more than one fun-loving fellow!

✦

Put together a co-ed softball team and join a league . . . or challenge another company to a friendly game of slo-pitch. The more fellows on the team, the better off you'll be. Plan to practice once or twice a week and, of course, afterwards go somewhere for beer and pizza.

✦

Plan a company activity or weekend getaway . . . like attending a local sporting event, bicycle riding, a gambling junket, skiing, camping trip, or a weekend at the lake. The more appealing to men, the more likely they'll participate.

✦

Assemble volunteers to pick up trash. Get your company's name on a highway sign acknowledging the group's help in keeping that part of the road clean. Make arrangements to do this at least once a month. After the work is done, go somewhere for lunch or dinner and reward yourselves for a job well done!

✦ ✦ ✦

BUSINESS ACTIVITIES . . .

There are a wide variety of business and professional associations that meet frequently and welcome guests or new members. When checking out an organization or pre-registering for a function, find out the ratio of men to women. Unless it is something you need to attend, do not waste your time if attendees are predominately female. Remember, you're looking for opportunities where the guys outnumber the gals.

At seminars and meetings, do not take a seat until knowing who will be sitting next to you. It's better to choose who you sit next to, instead of the other way around. Also, pass out lots of business or personal cards. Everyone you meet should receive some information about your interests or what you do for a living and how to contact you.

The following suggestions will assist you in finding business opportunities where males are prevalent.

Find a seminar to attend. There are a multitude of seminars offered by many different groups and agencies. If you keep the subject matter within the marketing and business realm, the greater the likelihood of finding more male than female attendees. But you'll see, once you get there!

✦

Become involved with Kiwanis and Rotary clubs. Members of these national service organizations include active or retired business executives and professionals . . . *and 85% are men!* (At one time these clubs were exclusively male, but in recent years have opened their membership to women.) Not only does this have fantastic social potential, but these groups also do a lot of community service work. They meet on a regular basis and new members are always welcome . . . so, what are you waiting for?

✦

Locate a business networking group . . . and interact with businessmen at weekly or monthly breakfast and dinner meetings. There are many associations, like LeTip and Business Network International, with chapters throughout the country. However, check into the demographics before you attend a meeting expecting to see a lot of men – in some areas of the country one chapter may be mostly male, in others mainly female.

✦

Attend Chamber of Commerce functions. This organization is made up of businesses within a specific locale. In addition to men outnumbering the women, this is a wonderful opportunity to make business and social contacts at frequent meetings and mixers. Anyone involved in a commercial enterprise may join. So, sign up and represent your employer . . . this may be the one idea that works for you!

✦

Patronize restaurants with banquet facilities. Find out ahead of time when functions are scheduled. Then wait in the bar until after the event is over for a chance meeting with those who decide to stick around for a nightcap. You can also poke your head in, if it looks like there's potential, ask if guests are welcome and when the next get-together will be held. Then put it on your calendar and be sure to go!

✦

Be involved in Toastmasters. Men are often the majority in this public speaking group. Gatherings are held weekly, as members help each other perfect their communication skills. Stop by one of their meetings . . . you'll be pleasantly surprised at who is there!

✦

Join a speakers bureau. For those of you with a motivational message you'd like to share or who are knowledgeable on a particular subject, this organization will locate groups that may be interested in your keynote speech. One friend, a school teacher, was extremely successful meeting men by giving motivational speeches to a variety of business groups. Find the nearest office in the *Yellow Pages*™ under "Speakers Bureau" or get a comprehensive list of organizations by searching the Internet.

✦

Wander around a trade show or convention. There are numerous industry sponsored expositions that businessmen attend. Check with local exhibition sites or the Internet, where you will find a very good website, ***www.tscentral.com***, containing information on trade shows, conventions and seminars for a variety of organizations and industry groups, both nationally and internationally. Don't pass up this super opportunity to meet both male vendors and show goers.

✦

Get a temporary job with a trade show exhibitor. If you work in one of the booths, you will have a chance to talk with hundreds of convention goers. When an exhibition is scheduled at a location near you, contact the sponsoring group for a list of vendors. Exhibitors will often hire local individuals to help out at these venues. It's worth a try!

✦

Frequent hotels and restaurants near convention sites. Show goers and vendors often stay in hotels and dine close to where the function is being held. After hours will find them entertaining clients or unwinding in one of the restaurants or lounges. I know it's hard to believe, but these fellows have been known to have a lot of fun when on the road!

✦

Become a daytrader. Many investment firms are offering this new form of stock market trading to their clients. After a comprehensive training session on system use and transaction how-tos, investors can sit at computer terminals and actively participate in the day's Wall Street activity. Very few women are involved in this pastime and if you have the wherewithal you may want to consider this. If nothing else, at least go through the training class . . . you'll be glad you did!

✦

Enroll in an investment class. Learn about stocks and bonds and other opportunities for a secure future. At the same time meet other like-minded people, particularly gentlemen looking for growth and protection of their assets.

✦

Participate in an investment club. These groups pool together members monies to make collective investments that the club has researched and decided to participate in. Many of the early groups were predominately female, so ask up front about membership. And, if you decide to start a group, gear it to male executives or retirees.

✦ ✦ ✦

THE HOME FRONT

Do you know who lives three, four, or even five blocks away from you? If you are like most people, you only know a few of your neighbors. Once you get out and meet those who live nearby, you will be surprised to find out who's been right under your nose all this time. I can't tell you how many times I've met someone at a function, only to discover that he lived within a few blocks of me!

Now let's look at some of the available options that are closer to home.

Give some thought to where you live. Investigate other areas of the country which have more unattached men per capita than women. Cities near military bases and college towns usually have a high concentration of males, as do outdoor recreational areas and high-technology corridors. As an example, I recently read that the Silicon Valley community of San Jose had a surplus of 5,500 unmarried men. If you're willing to relocate, this may be the place to go! Additionally, females are currently outnumbered by single males in three states – Alaska, Hawaii and Nevada. If all else fails, you may want to relocate to one of these areas, or at least spend a little time there . . . it could very well change your luck!

✦

Consider moving to a new residential complex. If you have not met anyone interesting where you currently live, a location change might make all the difference in the world! When choosing a new apartment, keep the following in mind:
  • *Location* – is it near a high activity area, such as a popular recreational spot or downtown commercial district.

- *Who lives there* – get some demographic data from the property manager, like ratio of men to women, ages, professions and what percentage are single. The more unattached men in your age group, the better it is for you.
- *Look for amenities that are appealing to men* – like a weight room and sports courts. Ask to use them for a short period of time to get a feel for the complex. This is your chance to scope out the male population and determine if that is where you'd like to live.
- *Are the tenants active?* Lots of activities = more new friendships.
- *Notice cars in parking stalls* – particularly automobiles that men drive, such as pickup trucks, four-wheel drives and sports cars.

✦

Spend a weekend apartment hunting . . . even if you don't plan to move. You are only "pretending" to look. What you really want is permission to use the facilities for a week or two. This way you can meet many of the residents without having to commit to a lease.

✦

Get a roommate or move in with someone . . . especially if you live by yourself. Not only will you have someone around to talk to, but this will instantly expand your circle of friends.

✦

Advertise for a male roommate. This is a great way to meet a lot of fellows. Do this whether you want one or not! Not only will you have a captive audience, but you can be specific about what you are looking for: "Non-smoking, professional, male roommate, 30 - 40." (Be sure to give an age range, you don't want to waste your time interviewing "twenty somethings," especially if you're in your forties.) Focus on men who are outgoing with lots of interests. They probably will have many male friends, as opposed to the new guy in town who has yet to meet anyone. By the way, you don't have to share your home with anyone until you find the right fit. For obvious reasons, before interviewing someone or giving them your address, check out their references. Then meet them for the first time in a neighborhood coffee shop. Remember, safety first!

✦

Answer a "looking for female roommate" ad. Some males who live together like having a woman around. Respond to those who are similar in age, background and/or interests. Again, be cautious and meet them at a public place rather than walking into an uncomfortable situation.

✦ ✦ ✦

MEET YOUR NEIGHBORS . . .

Start a betting pool. If you live in a residential complex, this is an easy way to meet male occupants. Go door-to-door asking each male resident, if he wants to be involved (you'll find that most men will). I guarantee, after several weeks of this, you will be on friendly terms with quite a few guys!

✦

Be neighborly. Bake some cookies or a casserole and take the "leftovers" to a male neighbor. What better way to say, "I like you!"

✦

Pick up your mail around the same time each day . . . and hang around the lobby while you read it. With any kind of luck, that fellow you've had your eye on will be stopping by for his mail, too.

✦

Use the swimming pool. In many apartment complexes this is the main social hub for residents. Even though the gals will outnumber the guys, that's okay, because anyone of them may have a friend who is just right for you!

✦

When you have clothes to wash, hang around the laundry room. If you live in an apartment, you know that most residents go back to their units between cycles. If you want to meet male tenants, you've got to be there when they pop in and out.

✦

Spend an afternoon washing and waxing your car. This will get you outside where you can interact with neighbors and visitors as they come and go. Besides, this beats sitting inside and you'll have the shiniest car on the block!

✦

Help a charity. Go door-to-door asking for contributions and meet your neighbors while offering assistance to a worthwhile cause. This will also give you a chance to come in contact with individuals who live within a few blocks of you that you have not yet met. Be sure to get the number of any men you meet, so they can be included in your next affair.

✦

Do something unusual to attract the attention of someone who lives nearby. Place something whimsical on your deck or in your yard, like an unusual piece of sculpture, or put up a placard on some controversial issue you feel strongly about . . . and then see what your neighbor has to say!

✦

Set up a service single men in your complex or neighborhood would use. Think of things that will not take too much of your time, that you can do along with your daily routine, like:
  • *Preparing home cooked meals* – just double or triple your casserole and pasta recipes.
  • *Watering and tending to houseplants* – arrange one or two visits a week, but make sure he's home before you stop by . . . the more chances to visit with him, the better it will be.
  • *Pet sitting or walking* – busy professionals cannot always get home in time to take the pooch out. Besides, how can he not love you for taking such interest in his best friend?

✦

Put out a community newsflyer . . . a great way to get to know those who live in your vicinity. Visit with residents in the complex or neighborhood, letting them know what you're doing. Find out their interests or any issues they may have and include announcements or services needed, like garage sales or watering plants when individuals are out-of-town. Put all of this in the newsletter and distribute on a monthly basis.

✦

Organize a neighborhood watch. The idea is to keep an eye out for each other, especially when no one is at home. Have an introductory meeting to get to know those around you. And then, you'll have a reason to contact the bachelor down the street.

✦

Call someone who lives alone. Invite him to join you for dinner, a concert, or a walk around the neighborhood. There's no harm in trying and he may return the favor!

✦

Whenever you call on a male neighbor who is not home . . . leave a note with why you came by, like a football pool or upcoming party, and suggest he stop by your place for more details . . . the rest I'll leave up to you!

✦

Get up early and go outside. Do things in the mornings around your neighborhood – not only is there a whole world of people out there you may be unaware of, you'll also find early risers are very friendly. Walk or jog the same route at the same time each day. Once you establish a routine, you will start seeing familiar faces. As I've previously mentioned, many of my close friendships started this way.

✦

Sit in front of your home and visit with passers-by. If you have a front porch, get a comfortable rocker or hang a swing and spend some time in it. Once you get to know an individual who passes by frequently, invite him to join you for a toddy or a little chitchat. There's no harm in asking and it may be all that is needed to get him to notice you.

✦ ✦ ✦

GET-TOGETHERS ...

Find several neighbors for a specialty group. Talk to male residents who live in the area about their interests and then organize a few activities for their participation. Try one of the suggestions below and see who joins in:
  • *Card or game club* – such as Poker, Cribbage, or Chess.
  • *Exercise group* – for daily runs or calisthenics.
  • *Computer users* – exchange freeware, discuss technical problems, or help each other learn different application programs.
  • *Travel adventures* – organize weekend and vacation getaways.
  • *Sports group* – attend athletic events and participate in different sporting activities, like kayaking, skiing and scuba diving.

✦

Organize functions that bring your neighbors together. Remember, when you are the organizer, you have the potential to meet a larger number of people. Concentrate on activities men are interested in, like attending an R&B concert, viewing a car race, or cheering on a local sports team.

✦

Go door-to-door ... with information on activities or groups that you are organizing. This also gives you a chance to introduce yourself and chat with each neighbor. And be sure to get their phone number, particularly the men, so you contact them at a later time.

✦

When you meet a new male neighbor ... find a reason to be in touch with him again. For example, invite him to an informal get-together to meet a few neighbors or include him in one of the many activities you are involved. And, of course, if he has any single buddies, have him bring them, too.

✦

Buy an old pinball machine ... and invite someone who lives nearby to come over and play it. Not only is this a great ice breaker, but he will want to come over again and again to hone his flipper skills!

✦

Extend an open invitation for dinner. This is a great opportunity for apartment dwellers and those who work or associate with numerous unattached men. Send out invitations and/or put up notices in your building, for example, "Join me for homemade spaghetti the first Tuesday of every month at 6:30 p.m." Now all you have to do is make plenty of pasta and wait for the guys to come by! Once you see how successful this is, you may want to set aside the same night every week. Not only will men pop in and out from week to week, they will also tell their friends, who will tell their buddies, and before you know it, you'll have more fellows than you'll know what to do with!

✦

Coordinate a Sunday brunch bicycle ride. Get a group together and peddle to a favorite eatery. If there are more than ten of you, let the restaurant know ahead of time, so they will be prepared for the group. And for those who want to continue on after brunch, there will be many more places where the group can stop. This became so popular in a beach community where I was living, that we were forced to curtail the event when more than fifty bikers clogged up the main city thoroughfare. It could turn out to be a big hit for you, too!

✦

Plan a progressive dinner party. Ask several neighbors who you'd like to know better to be a part of this. The idea is to go from house-to-house with each location offering a different course of the meal. One of my most memorable parties was with a group of fellows that lived a few blocks from me – they brought the guys and I invited the gals. In retrospect, we must have been quite a sight – about 35-40 of us walking the several blocks between locations. Many strangers stopped to ask what we were doing and, of course, we invited them to join us. Consequently, the party got progressively larger as we proceeded. Here are suggested courses for a five-stop party:

- *First stop* - appetizers and drinks
- *Second stop* - salad
- *Third stop* - main course
- *Fourth stop* - dessert and after-dinner drinks
- *Fifth stop* - dancing and/or games

◆

Invite nearby residents for an informal soiree. Do something easy or spontaneous, like one of the following:

- *Welcome a new neighbor* – a great way to endear you to the new guy on the block.
- *Organize a potluck* – everyone brings some food or drink.
- *During inclimate weather have a picnic in front of your fireplace* – roast hot dogs and "s'mores."

◆

Close off the street and have a block party. Hire a band and dance or play games like volleyball, croquet and horseshoes. And if you live in an apartment, take the party to a nearby park. This may be so successful that it will become a frequent event.

◆

Sponsor a *Monday Night Football* party. Set up several TVs, have a betting pool and lots of food and drink. There are at least 17 weeks of MNF, so you'll have plenty of opportunities to get to know several new fellows.

◆ ◆ ◆

OTHER HABITATS . . .

Look for fire trucks in market parking lots. This means there are several firemen inside shopping. Stop the car and get in there . . . this is your chance to meet a couple of cuties!

◆

Grocery shop on weekends and evenings . . . when men are most likely to be there. It has been publicized in the media that markets are great places to meet singles. Unfortunately, not all grocery stores are equal. When it comes to finding unattached men, some are better than others – those near apartment complexes, colleges and recreational areas are your best bets. Notice what's in shopping carts, if it's piled high, he probably is buying for a family, few items usually means he is unattached and if a cart is filled with beer and chips, chances are very good there's a party nearby!

✦

Frequent restaurants and retail stores in areas singles live . . . near apartments, condominiums and other previously mentioned locales. Do all your shopping and errands there and increase your chances of meeting someone who lives close by. **$** If you are looking for a well-heeled gentleman, patronize places near upscale areas, even if it means going out of your way to get there.

✦

$ Walk through an area of expensive or stately homes. If you see someone interesting, engage him in a conversation. Inquire about the neighborhood, ask directions, or where there's a good place to have lunch nearby. Although single men don't always live in these neighborhoods, oftentimes they visit family or friends that do. And you just never know who you might bump into!

✦

$ Set up an account at a bank in an affluent neighborhood. Many people prefer banking close to where they live. So, the possibility of meeting someone of means is most probable when you bank where he does. And, of course, while you're waiting for a teller, be sure to visit with the gentleman behind you.

✦ ✦ ✦

8

WHERE THEY SPEND THEIR LEISURE

If you want to meet men *and* have a lot of them to choose from, you must get involved in things that interest them. The following suggestions focus on those activities which males spend a great deal of time pursuing.

CAR STUFF

Become a member of a car club. There are local groups for nearly every automobile made and it's not necessary to own a particular make of car, but you should have some knowledge of or a desire to acquire one some day. Activities include monthly meetings, parties, picnics and weekend caravans. There's also a great sense of comradery within these groups and members often get together for larger state and national events. Contact car dealerships for information on clubs in your area or research the Internet, which has information on thousands of auto organizations and activities.

Once you locate one or more clubs that you're interested in, find out when the meetings are and get a schedule of events. Include some of these activities in your database and then go to a few of them . . . you'll be glad you did!

✦

Find a car show to attend. Every year there are thousands of exhibits throughout the country, ranging in size from small club showings to huge events drawing tens of thousands of people. At a local level, look for weekend shows, which are often held at parks, drive-in restaurants, hotels and other locations with large parking lots. You will also discover that the type of car generally determines the interested age group – classic or vintage autos (cars over 25 years old) are preferred by older gentlemen, hot rods by younger fellows. Walk around and admire the old autos and the loving care with which they've been maintained and restored. Strike up a conversation with a car's owner, he will love talking about his pride and joy. A few questions to get the dialog going: "I've never seen anything quite like this, what makes it so different?" "How much restoration have you done?" "Are you the original owner?"

✦

$ Become acquainted with expensive or classic cars. If you're looking for someone with money you should be able to recognize the high-performance automobiles they drive and/or collect, such as Porsche, Ferrari, Corvette, Lamborghini and Bugatti. Familiarize yourself with these autos by talking with knowledgeable male friends or picking up a couple of good books on the subject and browsing through car magazines. Your public library will not only have several volumes, but also many periodicals, including years of back issues to bring you up-to-speed . . . no pun intended!

✦

$ Dress up and attend a Concours d'elegance. This is the cream of the crop for vintage automobile collectors and is well attended by gentlemen of means. The granddaddy of them all is at Pebble Beach on California's Monterey Peninsula and is usually held the third week of August. In addition to lots of men, there will be auctions, races and other exhibits in conjunction with the Concours. Since many car enthusiasts travel long distances to attend these shows, patronizing nearby hotels and restaurants is a must.

✦

$ Attend a car auction. No doubt about it, if there will be hard-to-find and expensive automobiles up for sale, there will be lots of affluent gentlemen. One of the larger and better-known events is the annual Barrett-Jackson Classic Car Auction held during January in Scottsdale, Arizona. If you are looking for rich men, get yourself gussied up, as this is one event you should not miss!

✦

$ Answer an ad for a vintage automobile for sale. This is a super way to spend some one-on-one time with a man, both on the phone and later when looking at the car. *But be forewarned, you should know something about the automobile before trying this, otherwise you will be fooling no one.* You can also find out if he is married or not, by asking questions about the auto and then following up with, "Does your wife drive this car or are you the main driver?"

✦

$ Test drive a Ferrari . . . or other high-end automobile. But be sure to dress as though you can afford one – these high-performance machines can cost well into the six-figure range and you want to look your best when you meet one of these well-off Ferrari autophiles.

✦

Consider purchasing an old classic. No matter where you go, men will stop and want to talk to you about the car. Plus, you can show it off at auto shows and meet all sorts of men . . . talk about your male magnet!

✦

Get involved in automobile racing. Motorsport racing is watched by more people than any other spectator sport in the world. And guess what . . . the majority of these onlookers are male! There are countless racing venues across America offering everything from destruction derby and drag racing to stock cars and CART racing. Road races are generally held during daylight hours, drag racing and destruction derby at night. Another plus, you can go by yourself and easily blend in with the crowd, either observing the competition from the grandstands or from numerous vantage points along the track. But wherever you go, there will be gorgeous men everywhere. If you've never thought to look for men at an automobile race, do yourself a favor and go . . . you won't regret it!

✦

Pass the time in an automotive museum. Men of all ages love looking at vintage autos and after a couple of hours, you are bound to meet at least one interesting gentleman!

✦

$ Go to a performance driving school. There are many institutes around the country geared toward racing enthusiasts and the art of defensive driving. Males far outnumber females at these facilities, especially the racing clinics. Once you complete the course, not only will you be prepared for most driving conditions and emergencies, but you also will have met many exciting men. As an aside, if you happen to have any teenage drivers, this is an excellent way for them to learn how to handle a car in difficult situations, giving you a little more peace of mind when they are out with the family automobile.

✦ ✦ ✦

HIGH FLYERS

$ Learn to fly. It takes time and money to earn a pilot's license, but the rewards are well worth it, as you come in contact with many well-to-do individuals. A cheaper alternative to fixed wing lessons is glider flying. If you have the wherewithal . . . by all means do it!

✦

$ Have breakfast or lunch at a municipal airport. Many small-craft landing fields have restaurant and/or lounge facilities for their customers. This is where most pilots relax while their planes are being refueled or readied for take off and offers many possibilities to meet aeronautical fellows.

✦

Attend a vintage fly-in or air show. There are several across the continent that attract thousands of male enthusiasts. But by far, the largest aviation show in the world is held in Oshkosh, Wisconsin, during the last week of July. With over 800,000 spectators and nearly 11,000 airplanes and pilots, this is one event you can't miss!

✦

Make your first jump at a skydiving school. Not only will you spend the day with a group of male trainees prior to taking your maiden jump, but you older gals will also find many seniors doing this, particularly to celebrate monumental birthdays.

✦ ✦ ✦

THEIR HOBBIES

Spend time in a hobby shop. You may think this is just for young boys, but don't be fooled, men of all ages never outgrow their love of collecting and putting together scaled models. Additionally, you will also find plenty of male enthusiasts in stores that specialize in remote controlled (RC) models. These include automobiles, airplanes and boats with small motors that are operated by radio frequency. While you're browsing, look for a train set to put under the Christmas tree or a model to assemble.

✦

Get involved with scale model clubs. Even though model building is thought of as a boy-thing, there are plenty of adult males, especially in groups that specialize in trains and airplanes. And the best part of all, you will be surrounded by men . . . can you think of anything better?

✦

Attend a model train show. Again, contrary to what you may think, it's not young boys, but adult males that are the main patrons at these exhibitions. You will see dozens of layouts where HO-scale trains travel through miniature environments, representing thousands of hours of work. Talk with the owners about their creations – it's why they're there. So, get yourself over there and talk to a few of these train guys and see where it leads!

✦

Make small-scale train accessories . . . a great opportunity for women who enjoy working with their hands. This will put you in touch with male hobbyists who may not have the time to create their own realistic miniatures and you'll bring in some added income, too.

✦

Look for men flying RC airplanes . . . in parks, football fields and other open spaces. Contact hobby shops or model airplane clubs to find out where these remote controlled models are flown locally. Plus, there also are more than 1,000 competitions around the country . . . anyone of which could find the man you've been looking for!

✦

Start a hobby of male collectibles. If you frequent specialty stores, antique shops and swap meets looking for treasures, you will meet many fellows who share the same interest. Any involvement with the following will put you around male collectors:
   • *Trains, airplanes, boats and automobiles*
   • *History* – particularly war memorabilia
   • *Sports* – trading cards and autographed mementos
   • *Guns and knives*
   • *Tobacco pipes*
   • *James Bond souvenirs and memorabilia*
   • *Western paraphernalia and artifacts*

✦ ✦ ✦

THEY GOTTA HAVE MUSIC

Attend a blues or sixties rock concert. These are two of the most popular kinds of music men enjoy listening to, particularly baby boomers who were in college when this music was at its peak. With the resurgence of sixties rock 'n' roll groups, you're sure to see a lot of gray beards and ponytails!

✦

Listen to lounge entertainment at a hotel. This is a relaxed environment for listening to live music . . . and it is not uncommon to meet a male guest or two.

✦

Browse through a guitar shop. Americans purchase more than one million guitars every year and guess who buys the majority of them? The only problem, if you don't play there isn't much to do except look at the different kinds of guitars on display. Many shops also carry violins and if you "pretend" you are interested in one of them, you can stay awhile and see who else comes in. In any event, while you're there, if you see someone strumming on a *Stratocaster*, hang around and listen to him play and then comment on how nice he sounds – any "stringer" will love hearing how good he is.

✦

Look for vintage guitar shows. Used guitar swap meets are *immensely* popular with guys of all ages. The last one I attended was inundated with hundreds of guitarists and guess what . . . only a handful were females!

✦

Rent a musical instrument and learn to play. Again, the most popular with male musicians are guitars. Other instruments to consider are harmonicas, drums and horns. If you stick with one of these four instruments, there probably won't be a gal within sight! Check music shops or a local community college for musical instruction classes.

✦

If you're a pianist, consider playing a synthesizer. You will sometimes find synths at the same places that sell guitars, which will give you a chance to meet both guitarists and keyboardists. Go to as many in-store seminars or classes as you can find, they will be heavily attended by musical guys.

✦

Answer an ad for "singer wanted" . . . that is, if you can carry a tune! Here is a great way to meet others with a passion for music. Not only will you become friendly with the fellows in the band, but also their pals and the people you'll meet at different gigs.

✦

Locate a practice studio. This is your chance to jam with the guys. Any woman with musical talent will find lots of men to interact with during practice sessions. If there's one around, your local guitar shop will know about it.

✦

Arrange for a small combo to play in front of your house or apartment. Get a few friends together or hire a few musicians to entertain on a Saturday afternoon. This will surely draw a crowd . . . and get the attention of any men who live nearby!

✦ ✦ ✦

THEY ARE GAMBLERS

Men comprise the majority of gamblers, especially at casinos and racetracks. Any occasion you have to take part in one or more of the following activities will be well worth the effort.

CASINOS . . .

Visit a gambling casino. This has tremendous possibilities for meeting people of all ages and backgrounds. Even if you are not a gambler, there are many other things to do, like enjoying the lounge shows and top-name entertainment, dining in a variety of restaurants, or just watching the activity. If no casinos are close by, seek out well-known destinations, such as Las Vegas, Reno and Atlantic City or other locations around the country and across the border in Canada.

✦

Learn to shoot craps. Craps is extremely popular with men and unless you know how to play, this dice game can be very intimidating to the novice. Locate an empty table or one where only a few people are playing and ask the croupier or other table personnel to help you with the nuances of the game, they'll be glad to help. Then, not only will you be comfortable walking up to a table and placing a bet, but also visiting with the "high-roller" next to you.

✦

Squeeze between two men playing craps. Now you've got two fellows to interact with. And, if you're lucky and throw a lot of winning numbers, you may have several fans before the night is over! **$** When looking for men of means, notice those with a pile of black chips in front of them . . . they're worth $100 each!

✦

Sit next to a fellow at the Blackjack table. This is a super way to meet men and possibly win a little money at the same time. One of the most social of all games of chance, you can play for hours, while conversing with other players at the table. You will meet many interesting gentlemen this way. If you don't believe me . . . give it a try!

✦

$ Look for "high-roller" tables and other designated spots for big spenders. These areas are set aside for gamblers, usually men, who bet large sums of money and are accorded some privacy or separation from the rest of the casino patrons. Some are off limits to the public, but you can still watch from outside and take note of who is playing. Once someone leaves, see where he goes – probably somewhere else to gamble – and then place yourself in a position to make his acquaintance.

✦

Wander around the slot machines until you see someone of interest . . . and then go over and play the machine next to him. You can always start the conversation by asking how he's doing and before long you may find you have more in common than just gambling!

✦

Sit at the bar and play the slots. You will frequently find men at the bar taking a break from gambling or enjoying a sporting event on television. Find a seat next to a nice looking gent and try your luck . . . and I don't mean with the slot machine!

✦

Relax in the "sports book." In addition to off-track betting on horse races and college or professional sports, many men use this area as a respite from the din of the casino. Most of the betting activity is on current horse races around the country, but you can also place bets on who will win the Super Bowl and other sporting events. Seating is informal, so sit beside whoever looks interesting . . . and the rest is up to you!

✦

$ Learn to play Baccarat. Made popular by James Bond and played by the rich and famous, particularly those who also gamble in Europe. Although players are often sequestered into private rooms, you can usually observe them from a distance through glass windows. If you have the *chutzpah*, learn this game and meet the wealthiest of gentlemen.

✦ ✦ ✦

RACETRACKS . . .

Cheer for a long shot at the horse races. Make no mistake, males are the main attendees at the racetrack, especially during the week. If you've ever wondered where to meet men during the day . . . this is where you'll find them! Arrive early, as most seating is on a first come, first served basis, however, there are many places to sit or stand, even if you do not purchase grandstand or the nicer clubhouse seating. But whenever and wherever you go, there will be lots of men around . . . so take advantage of it!

✦

Interact with those around you . . . there will be lots of time between races, so talk with the fellow standing in front of you or sitting next to you, "Who do you like in the next race?" is a good start. People will always be eager to tell you what horses they've chosen, and vice versa. When it comes time to wagering on your race selections, you will also spend a lot of time standing in line . . . and you know what that means! **$** There are several betting locations, some are more accessible to the affluent than others, so place your bets near expensive box-seats or Turf Club seating.

✦

Notice where men of interest are sitting . . . and find a spot nearby. Also, look for groups of buddies, the closer you are to the guys, the more likely you are to interact with them.

✦

$ Reserve a table in the clubhouse. This is a popular location for affluent track-goers to enjoy the races. Since seating is at a premium, reservations must be made several days in advance. If reserving a table for one, you may be asked if other individuals can be seated with you, if not, suggest that they do so, particularly male guests. This is very effective during the week when many gentlemen will be there by themselves.

✦

Even if you do not want to bet, you can enjoy the beauty of the horses and the ambiance of the track. There are many places to eat, sun yourself, or just people watch. Use this time to wander around and chat with as many fellows as you'd like.

✦

Bring a beach chair and sit by the track. Many track-goers come in groups and picnic in designated areas, so find a fun bunch to sit near and enjoy yourself.

✦

Ask the fellow next to you how to read *The Racing Form* **. . .** especially if you aren't familiar with one. This publication is a history of each thoroughbred's previous racing experience and is what most individuals use to determine which horses to wager on in each race. You can also pick one up ahead of time at a liquor store or mini-market within the track vicinity.

✦

$ Wander around by the paddocks . . . and watch the presentation of thoroughbreds before heading out to the track. This is where the owners and trainers come together with the jockeys for final instructions and saddling up and is your best chance to come in contact with the owners.

✦

Attend a tipster's a.m. briefing. Each morning prior to the first race, several horse handicappers will, for a fee, share their expertise and give you their Exacta and Daily Double choices for the day. Not only will you be surrounded by men, but you also will have enough information to pick a longshot. By the way, most of these fellows will be at the track later, so if someone catches your eye, be sure to sit next to him . . . and you may end up a winner, too!

✦ ✦ ✦

OTHER GAMING OPPORTUNITIES . . .

Set sail on a gambling cruise. Several cruise lines and Mississippi River boats offer gambling on the water. Not only is this a lot of fun, but you can count on there being plenty of unattached men aboard.

✦

Pick a horse at an off-track betting parlor. Racetracks usually offer parimutuel wagering after the local racing season has ended, which gives gamblers a chance to place bets on races around the country. As with all gaming establishments, you can get food and beverages while you enjoy the ambiance of this predominately male environment.

✦

Visit a poker parlor or card club. Yet another activity dominated by men. Card parlors are for the serious player, so be prepared – if you don't understand the game, don't play! Leave that to those who do. Instead sit at the bar while you watch the cardsharps.

✦

Get involved in a fantasy league. This is one of the fastest growing segments of the sports world with new groups starting up every day. Very few women participate and there are numerous opportunities to come in contact with other players. If you follow one of the three major sports or have any sports acumen, this is a fabulous way to meet guys and I highly suggest giving this a try. The league format is too complex to explain here, but there are magazines and plenty of information on the Internet regarding rules and how the leagues are structured. Basically, each participant is like a real owner of a team, he drafts and trades players and receives points based on how each of his players does during the week. At the end of the season the owner with the most team points wins. If you consider taking part in a league, be prepared to spend a lot of time and effort, as most participants will not appreciate individuals who do not take this seriously.

✦ ✦ ✦

GROUP INVOLVEMENT

Many unmarried men have the same problem as you . . . wondering where to meet someone of the opposite sex. If given the opportunity, most will jump at the chance of doing fun things with several like-minded singles. Not only does this relieve everyone of social pressures, but it also enables participants to get to know each other while doing something enjoyable in a relaxed environment. Plus, nothing breaks the ice between people better than sharing a common interest.

As a general rule, the greatest number of males are in business, sports and certain specialty clubs. The following suggestions will help you discover those groups where men are prevalent. Get involved in one of these and see what transpires.

Join a special interest group. There are thousands of national and local organizations in which you can take part and meet other people with similar interests. Before joining a group, however, find out how many men are members. Obviously, if your goal is to meet the opposite sex, you want to be involved with those that have a lot of male participants. To discover which clubs are available in your area, look in the "Calendar" section of the newspaper and the *Yellow Pages*™ or contact specialty stores for related clubs they may know about. And, of course, go online where there is a tremendous amount of data on every imaginable organization, many with local connections.

✦

Be in charge of a club newsletter. Not only will this keep you personally in touch with everyone, but it also can be passed on to others who may be interested in joining. Besides, the most popular person is the one with all the news!

✦

Participate in a singles group. Emphasis is on organized outings and activities, such as weekend trips, sporting events, bicycling, dinners, dancing, camping and other social functions . . . the more adventuresome or male-oriented the activities, the more fellows in the group.

✦

$ Get a membership in a private social group. The cost is well worth it as you begin meeting many well-off, highly successful members. Normally classified as non-profit organizations, these exclusive clubs must register with the city or state to operate. To locate private clubs in your area, contact the appropriate regulatory agency to get a list of these groups.

✦

Find out which of your friends or colleagues belong to private organizations . . . especially sports and yacht clubs and ask to join them for dinner or include you in some activity at the club. And be sure to return the favor . . . you may be thanking them for more than you think!

✦

Take an IQ test and become a Mensa member. There are far more men than women in this international group of intellectuals, but you must first take an IQ test and score in the top 2% of the general population. Contact a local chapter of American Mensa for more details.

✦

Get involved in a local *Magic: the Gathering* club. This relatively new strategy game is becoming increasingly popular with young men in their twenties and thirties. Hobby shops and adult game outlets will have more details on meetings and tournaments. If nothing else, go to a "gathering" and see how this fascinating game is played.

✦

Locate a chess club to join. You won't be disappointed, as males are the overwhelming majority in board game groups. Check with game stores for information on local clubs. Once again, if you don't know how to play, find a friend to teach you or get some help from other members. There also are several good computer programs to help you learn the game.

✦

Join a booster group. All colleges with a major sports program have booster clubs and their main purpose is to heighten enthusiasm and raise money for their teams. Many alumni belong to these organizations, but anyone who wants to support a college's sports program can participate. Additionally, club members often sit together in designated areas, particularly at football games, which is the most popular with supporters. They are a fun group, so check it out!

✦ ✦ ✦

SPIRITUALITY . . .

Get involved in a religious singles organization. There are many affiliates throughout the nation with ties to one denomination or another. A comprehensive list of groups is also available via the Internet, including two of the most active – the Jewish Singles Connection and the Catholic Singles Network. There are many trips and activities available at both the local level and with other interested individuals from around the country. If you're looking for a spiritual guy, this may be the answer.

✦

Be part of a singles group at your church. Although there will be many more ladies than men, don't forget that everyone you meet, both male and female, may have a bachelor friend or neighbor who is just right for you!

◆

Find a Buddhist group to join. For those with an interest in this spiritual community, you will discover that males outnumber the women by quite a bit. If nothing else, go to a meeting and get another point of view, it certainly can't hurt.

◆

$ Attend church near wealthy neighborhoods. There are many opportunities within the church to volunteer your time and meet other parishioners. Get to know the congregation by joining a group, attending a retreat, or taking part in other social functions. Besides, what better way to meet a man of means!

◆

Patronize hotels near a Promise Keepers convention. This is a gathering of Christian men whose goal is to promote spiritual awareness within their homes, churches and communities. Tens of thousands of men attend these affairs and although a majority of these fellows are married, many are not. Remember, all it takes is one!

◆ ◆ ◆

STARTING A GROUP . . .

If you can't find a special interest group to join, start one of your own. And since you are the one putting it together, you can determine who to gear the group toward. If you want men, advertise the fact . . . "Men needed for bridge group" or "Men interested in a gourmet dining club, please contact . . ."

Plan to meet at least once a month, if not more frequently. And to get the word out on your new club, advertise on the Internet, in local publications, or send information to a newspaper's social or activities editor and include something that can be put in an article or calendar listing. You also may want to put up notices in office buildings, apartment complexes, sports clubs and retail stores associated with your group's specialty.

♦ ♦ ♦

LEARN SOMETHING NEW

Seminars and classes are a wonderful way to meet males of all ages. The secret is to attend those where you will be outnumbered by the opposite sex. This means seeking out the ones that are most appealing to men. Here are a few ideas that are worth a try:

Find out about available night classes at a local college or vocational school. There are a number of men taking business and special interest courses. Try one of the following and see who you meet:
- *Business* – starting a business, marketing, business finance, management and leadership skills
- *Computer* – Computer Aided Design (CAD), certification programs, network administration, programming, spreadsheet and database management
- *Financial* – income tax preparation, stock market investing, retirement planning and money management
- *General interest* – furniture refinishing, carpentry and bicycle maintenance
- *Liberal arts* – anthropology, philosophy, astronomy, geology and ancient history

♦

Learn to sculpt. You'll find more male artisans in physical mediums, like sculpting or pottery, than in basic drawing classes. By the way, I've known more than one artistic woman who's met her future spouse in a sculpting class. Maybe you will, too!

♦

Become well-versed in a foreign language . . . Spanish will have the most men, especially in regions of the country where communication with Hispanics is important. Also, Mexico and Central America are two popular destinations for single guys and speaking the language is helpful. Besides, one of them may need your help in conjugating his verbs!

✦

Take a woodworking class. Learn proper use of power tools and carpentry basics. Not only helpful for the self-sufficient woman, but you *will* be outnumbered by men. Check trade schools or community colleges for course information, as this is one class you'll be glad you signed up for!

✦

Sit in on a workshop at a home improvement center. Many males attend in-store demonstrations for such do-it-yourself tasks, as installing a ceramic tile floor, building a retaining wall, or changing an electrical outlet. Ask one of them to come over and give you a hand . . . it's worth a try!

✦

Adjust your carburetor in a car repair class . . . and I'll bet you'll be the only female! Besides, knowing more about your car can't hurt considering the amount of time we spend in them.

✦

Snap better pictures with a photography course. Learn professional photo techniques and how to develop your own film in a class where most of the students will be masculine. Invite a classmate to spend the day taking pictures with you or perhaps he can help you create a darkroom in your home.

✦

Save a life and learn CPR and mouth-to-mouth recessitation. These classes are usually taught by firemen . . . need I say more?

✦ ✦ ✦

TEACH A CLASS . . . FOR MEN ONLY

A great way to meet the opposite sex is to teach a class, but gear it to men only. If you have some expertise that you can teach a group of fellows, don't hesitate to do it! Find a location to hold your class, such as a community or senior center, an apartment complex clubhouse, the public library, or through a continuing education institution. Also, contact several local organizations, as they will often supply space if you teach their members.

Advertise in regional papers or specialty publications and focus your marketing to groups that may have an interest in your subject matter. You can also post notices where you work and live, at wine or liquor stores, fitness clubs and other places men frequent.

Here are a couple of class ideas you might try:

Quick and healthy cooking for the bachelor. Most men do not want to spend much time in the kitchen, so offer a few of your favorite recipes that can easily be prepared with commonly used ingredients.

✦

Learn a software application. If you are proficient with word processing or another popular program, here is an opportunity to share your knowledge and meet some men while you're at it.

✦

Conversational Spanish. As previously mentioned, Mexico and Latin American countries are very popular vacation spots for males. If you can teach phrases and common words that they can use, this will be a hit.

✦ ✦ ✦

COMPUTERS AND THE NET

Learn to use a computer. Many community colleges offer a variety of classes where you will learn everything from computer basics to network management. Be sure to sit next to a male classmate, or better yet, between two of them. Chances are very good you'll need each other's help as you work through problems you're bound to encounter.

✦

Take a programming or relational database class. Even if you don't understand it, you'll meet lots of guys in these predominately male classes. Besides, if you are having difficulty, you can ask one of the fellows to come over in the evening and help you with your class assignment.

✦

Join a computer user's group. Men far outnumber the women in this techie crowd, especially popular are Macintosh™ user groups. Contact local computer stores for more details on monthly meetings and other activities. Even if you are not a Mac user, I suggest you go to the meetings . . . when it comes to males, this is truly bonus, bonanza, bingo time!

✦

Communicate with a UseNet group on the Internet. There are thousands of these on everything imaginable, giving like-minded people a chance to interact with each other in chat rooms. You've probably heard about the many romantic connections being made over the Internet, this is where many of them begin. *Warning: do not be in a hurry to get together with individuals you meet this way, as there are many unsavory characters out there preying upon innocent victims – a situation you don't ever want to be in!*

✦

Create a personal website . . . include things you are fond of, your interests and any other pertinent information you'd like to share and then link it to several singles sites. You will have no control over who contacts you, but there is the likelihood you will communicate with individuals from around the world. But, please heed the previous warning and be aware of what you may be getting into if you give out too much personal information to total strangers.

✦

Register with an on-line dating service. There are many websites on the Internet where you enter personal information into a database and then are put in contact with others with similar interests. A few offer this as a free service, but the majority charge a fee. Try out one that gives you a free trial period and see what happens. On a whim, a business acquaintance tried this and is now engaged to the first man she met. Not only was it love at first sight, but it didn't cost her a cent!

✦ ✦ ✦

VOLUNTEERING

There are many opportunities to meet a variety of men when you volunteer your time and expertise to a non-profit or charitable group. Why not give one of the following suggestions a try:

Work on a Habitat for Humanity project. This is a favorite pastime for ex-President Jimmy Carter and his wife, Rosalynn. This non-profit organization builds low-income housing using donated time, money and supplies. Meet other charitable folks as you volunteer your weekends to paint, hammer nails, or other odd jobs. Oh, and did I mention . . . there will be lots of men!

✦

Give your assistance to youth organizations. Male volunteers are most often found helping youth groups, like inter-city and boy's clubs. Also, check with the United Way Volunteer Center for additional opportunities. **$** You will discover that involvement by professional athletes is very prevalent, especially with organizations that help under-privileged kids. Not only will you find this rewarding, but you also may find the man you've been wishing for!

✦

Discover volunteer opportunities through the Federal government. A few agencies with needs where men are prevalent are the Dept. of Interior, Fish and Wildlife Service, and National Park Service. To locate available options in your locale, look in the phone book under Federal listings for "Volunteer Opportunities."

✦

Become involved in an environmental group . . . like Greenpeace, which has lots of male supporters. Once you are committed to an issue that you feel strongly about, you will meet other like-minded individuals.

✦

$ Organize a charitable fund-raiser. Even though women often comprise the majority of committee members, many of the benefits and galas will be attended by well-to-do men and, because of your involvement, you will be in a position to meet many of them. Besides, what better way to make new friendships than working together on a mutual effort!

✦

$ Get involved in a local art museum association . . . and become a patron of the arts. Although many wealthy male contributors attend cultural activities, they often have dates. However, the more functions you take part in, the more gentlemen you will meet. And as you discover which ones are single, you can then invite one of them to attend an affair with you. It's worth a try!

✦

Help out at a shelter. These fellows may be down on their luck, but they are men just the same. Even though they are homeless or jobless, once they get back on their feet, they often will become viable prospects. We sometimes hear about successful entrepreneurs who were once down-and-out and one good turn changed their luck.

✦ ✦ ✦

THE POLITICAL ARENA

Be active in your local government. Sit in on a public meeting or get involved in a civic committee or citizen's group. Not only are these governing bodies comprised of a majority of men, but they also give you a chance to make friends with other concerned citizens. Once you are active in your community, you will meet more people than you can imagine. But, then, you won't know this, unless you do it!

✦

Run for office. Although the number of women entering the political arena is on the rise, men still outnumber the ladies. Whether your campaign is successful or not, you will be sought out by countless individuals and included in a variety of social functions, as the number of friends you make continues to grow.

✦

Help gather signatures for a petition. This is another super way to talk with individuals on environmental or political issues. Situate yourself in front of a home improvement center, sporting goods store, or other spot where there is a possibility of encountering men . . . and see who you meet! **$** If you want to find well-heeled gentlemen, station yourself outside a bank or coffeehouse in a high-end neighborhood.

✦

Busy yourself with a political event. There are many candidates at the local, state, or federal level that could use your help. Not only will you meet many male supporters while you campaign for your nominee, but you also will make dozens of new friendships . . . I guarantee it!

✦

Join a cause or demonstration . . . one that you feel strongly about. You will find, with the exception of women's issues, the vast majority of activists are male . . . and this just might be all the motivation you need!

✦

$ Get involved in a Political Action Committee (PAC). This is the money-gathering arm for many special interest organizations and the entity that is responsible for getting their issues before the lawmakers. And the majority of fund-raising events are attended by well-to-do entrepreneurs and corporate executives.

✦

Frequent places near your state capital. Men far outnumber women in government, so any restaurant, hotel and nearby business presents many opportunities to meet legislative and government personnel.

✦

$ Attend a meeting or session of your state or federal legislature. At this level of government, men comprise the majority of our leaders and their staff. Any occasion to patronize establishments near your state capitol or Washington, D.C., will have you hobnobbing with gentlemen in no time. One friend, who worked in the White House during Reagan's presidency, complained about being inundated by men at every turn. Are you thinking what I am . . . "Where do I go to sign up!"

✦ ✦ ✦

9

WHERE THEY RECREATE

Although the majority of males are either watching or participating in some sport or outdoor activity, most women have yet to figure out, if they get involved in these pastimes, they will meet men. The more sports you are involved in, either as a spectator or participant, the easier it will be to meet guys. It's as simple as that.

Give one of the following suggestions a try and see what ensues . . . the odds are with you!

PARTICIPATION SPORTS

GET INVOLVED WITH GOLF . . .

Okay, gals, this is where they are! I have found no other activity for individual participation where men are more prevalent than golf. According to the National Golf Foundation, the typical golfer is a

39-year-old male who makes $65,000 per year and plays one round of golf every other week . . . *and there are close to 19 million of them!* If you do nothing else, find a way to partake of this male candy store!

Visit a public golf course. During the week the best time to go is late afternoons when many golfers try to get in nine holes after work. On weekends anytime is good, as it will be extremely busy all day long. You'll also find many courses reserve one or two mornings a week for the exclusive use of their men's group, which means there will be lots of fellows on those days. While you're there, relax in the clubhouse, watch people practicing, or wander around the pro shop (this is where golfers get their tee times and where you can look at sportswear and accessories). Trust me . . . this is a good one!

✦

If you don't play the game, take lessons . . . you won't regret it! Most golf courses and driving ranges offer both individual and group lessons. Not only will you corporate gals begin to realize the importance of making business deals over a round of golf, but you also will be meeting lots of eligible men . . . so, get going!

✦

Hit a bucket of balls at the driving range. Almost all golf courses have facilities where you can practice hitting your woods and irons, and during the day, this is the best place to meet men while you work on your swing. But in the evenings and on weekends an independent range is usually your best bet – it will be absolutely packed with the opposite sex. While you practice, strike up a conversation with the fellow next to you, and if your swing needs improvement, ask for his help, almost all golfers will gladly offer pointers. If you don't have golf clubs, you can rent a set or try out new ones. Don't procrastinate . . . the sooner you get there, the sooner you will meet the man you've been looking for!

✦

Have something to eat in the clubhouse. Every public golf course has at least a snack bar and many have full-service restaurants.

Known as the "19th hole," they are very busy throughout the day while golfers socialize after completing their rounds. From the clubhouse or outside deck you can also watch golfers teeing off or hitting approach shots to the 9th and 18th greens. If there's a course near your office, by all means, spend your lunch hour there. In any event, stop by sometime during the weekend. Really . . . it doesn't get much better than this!

✦

Work on your putting and chipping at the practice green. Most golf courses have small greens near the clubhouse where golfers, prior to teeing off, work on their putting stroke and chip shots. You can do this, too, and it doesn't cost a cent!

✦

Take part in a ladies golf group. I don't advocate you spend all your time with the girls, but it will get you out to the course and ultimately around the boys. And remember, these gals may have bachelor friends, too!

✦

Ask the starter to place you with a threesome. If you already play golf, this is a fabulous way to meet lots of men. *But be forewarned: if you are a beginner, don't attempt this until you can hit the ball with some consistency. You don't want to alienate your group by holding them up!*

✦

$ Join a country club . . . if you can afford it! As with most golf groups, there are frequent functions and tournaments where you will meet other members. The more exclusive the club, the harder it is to join and, as you may have guessed, the more expensive, too. As an alternative, look into a social membership – you won't have access to the golf course, but you can partake of the social functions, which will put you around the members . . . and, it's a lot cheaper!

✦

Attend a professional golf tournament. There are two common ways to watch these competitions, either follow a particular golfer around the course or stay at one of the greens and watch all of them play through. Or you can do both and walk around with a group until you see a potential "target," then hang out there for awhile. In either case, there will be plenty of interesting men to talk with. If you want to meet the pros, attend one of the practice rounds when there are fewer spectators and the golfers have more freedom to visit with you. If you don't know anything about the sport, watch a professional golf tournament on television, which will help you learn the lingo and get some understanding of the game. And then, when you converse with a golfer you will know what he is talking about.

✦

Volunteer to help at a professional tournament. Contact the sponsoring group to offer your services. If you are selected, there will be many opportunities to meet both spectators and participants. Once your assignment is finished, you can enjoy the tournament and visit with some of the golf enthusiasts you've met.

✦

Help out at a club tournament. Public golf courses frequently host group tourneys. Check with the pro shop to see if assistance is needed, like driving the beer or sandwich carts . . . the golfers will love to see you coming!

✦

Find out when local tourneys are being held. This is a good time to be at the course, as participants will be milling around prior to the start of the tournament and after they have finished. Remember, it's just a matter of being at the right place at the right time!

✦

Station yourself at a 3-par and offer golfers a chance to "Hit the Green." This is an effective way to meet a lot of fellows and support a favorite charity at the same time. Here is how it works: pick the most difficult 3-par on the course, as golfers approach the hole, ask each one if he wants to "hit the green, double or nothing." If so, he contributes $5 and tries to hit his ball onto the green. If he succeeds, he gets double his money or $10. If he is unsuccessful, you keep his $5, which will be donated to a charity. The best part is you will get to talk with each group of guys as they play through. Oh, and don't worry about losing money, you *will* leave with a nice sum of cash.

✦

Get a part-time job at a driving range or country club ... and be around men all day long . . . what more can you ask?

✦ ✦ ✦

TENNIS AND BOWLING . . .

$ Join a tennis club. Similar to athletic clubs but the emphasis is on racquet activities. Although many men play tennis, there are far more women. However, if there are other amenities that appeal to men, like weight rooms and handball courts, there will be more male members.

✦

Look for public courts where men are playing. Check schools, parks and other outdoor tennis facilities. When you see two or more guys playing, stop and watch for awhile . . . and then see what happens!

✦

Practice your backhand and hit balls against a wall or a three-sided court. If someone is practicing by himself, ask if he'd like a partner. In any case, keep your eyes open for opportunities to meet other fellows who are recreating nearby, like a group of friends playing softball or someone out jogging. And . . . smile!

✦

$ Be a spectator at a professional tennis tournament. The larger, well-publicized contests will bring out celebrities and the well-to-do. So, head on over and see who's there!

✦

Watch a club tournament . . . at the recreation park or a local club. Many single parents will be rooting for their kids at youth tourneys. And, if a senior or men's competition is going on, you better stick around and watch the action. You can make it even more fun and cheer for your favorite!

✦

Spend time at a bowling alley . . . where there will be many good opportunities for male "sightings." Most have restaurants and cocktail lounges, plus plenty of seating to watch the bowlers. The best times to go are in the evenings and on weekends when the lanes are at their busiest.

✦

Join a co-ed league. This is a super way to meet lots of new folks. Find out when the next league is forming and get on a team. If it's too late to join one, put your name on a substitution list. Then whenever a team is missing a fourth bowler, you will be called to fill in. Not only will you have a chance to meet lots of different individuals, but you will also have way too much fun!

✦

If you don't know how to bowl, take lessons. In addition to being good exercise, it's not too strenuous and nearly anyone can do it. And then afterwards, hang around for awhile and see who comes in that catches your eye!

✦

Try bowling a few lines. If you have a choice of lanes, pick one adjacent to a group of fellows. Not only will you be instantly involved with them, but you will have a blast!

✦

After work watch the league bowlers . . . particularly men's groups. There are plenty of ways to meet male participants even if you are just spectating. So, pick out a few prospects and find a seat nearby and I'll bet before the night is over, you will have met at least one of them!

✦ ✦ ✦

BICYCLING . . .

Peddle along a busy bike path. Stop frequently and talk to other bikers or passers-by. Take along a knapsack of goodies and offer someone a snack or a thirst-quenching drink. This gesture may be all it takes for someone to notice you.

✦

Participate in a bicycle club and head out on a trek. This is a really great way to meet other cyclists and get fit at the same time. Check the "Calendar" section of the newspaper or bike shops for club information and weekend rides. Active groups will have something going on all the time . . . and so will you!

✦

Enter a bike race. Individuals at all ability levels participate in long distance rides and, of course, there will usually be more men than women. If you're not a racer, volunteer to be a part of the support group that follows the participants. Once you reach the destination, there will be lots of opportunities to meet the cyclists. Two-day rides, where an overnight stay is required, are best; then you will have additional time to interact with everyone.

✦

Get involved with a group of mountain bikers. This sport is extremely popular with men in their twenties and thirties. Once you find out where well-traveled trails are located . . . get yourself on over there!

✦

Bicycle around your neighborhood . . . on a nice evening or weekend afternoon. The goal is to ride up and down every street and see who you encounter that lives within a mile of you. You might be surprised at who is out watering his lawn or washing his car that you haven't yet met!

✦

Ride to areas where men are recreating . . . like the waterfront, ballfields, or any of the many locations mentioned throughout this chapter. Once you get there, stick around and watch what's going on. If you spot someone interesting, head on over in his direction . . . after that, you know what to do!

✦ ✦ ✦

OTHER SPORTS OPTIONS . . .

Start a boxing regime. As you spar with other pugilists, you will discover that not only is this a great way to get in shape, but there will be men everywhere. And while you're at it, see if one of them will help you with your punching bag technique.

✦

Earn your black belt in martial arts. The more physical the discipline, the greater number of male participants. Your best bets are self-defense classes, like Karate, Kung Fu and Judo. The non-violent or "centering" disciplines, like T'ai Chi and Aikido, will usually have more women.

✦

Take part in an active sports group . . . like a running, backpacking, or other outdoors club. The more activities you join in on, the more people you meet and the greater your chances of finding a meaningful relationship. It can happen . . . so, go do it!

✦

Get a free trial membership to a fitness club. Most will offer potential clients complimentary passes for a week or more. There is no obligation to join, so use this time to both exercise and meet as many new people as possible.

✦

Become a member of an athletic club. These differ from fitness chains in that they are more upscale and offer a lot more than exercise equipment and aerobics workouts, such as a restaurant, swimming pool, indoor track and racquet courts. Plus, there are ongoing club tournaments and social functions that you can be a part of and meet other members. **$** Generally, the more exclusive the club, the more affluent the men.

✦

Sign up for a racquetball match. Most athletic clubs have sign-up sheets so individuals can be paired with other solo players. Since males are the main participants of this fast-paced sport, your chances of getting placed with a man is very good. And for those of you who are unfamiliar with the game, it's easy to learn and you can have an enjoyable game with anyone at any skill level.

✦

Get involved with orienteering. This is timed land navigation with the aid of a topography map and compass. Going from point A to point B and using map landmarks, participants choose the best route to the next checkpoint. You can be as competitive as you want, either taking your time and strolling leisurely through your surroundings or completing it quickly and running the course. Men and women of all ages participate and demographics vary with each group. For more information contact a local chapter of the U.S. Orienteering Federation.

✦

Spend an hour at a popular jogging trail. As previously mentioned, this is one of my favorite ways to meet people. Plus, it doesn't cost anything and is something you can do by yourself. If you are not a runner, you can still enjoy the benefits of meeting people while you walk along the jogging path. Notice which trails are popular with male runners, particularly in the evenings after work, and go there around the same time every day. If you make a habit of doing this, you will begin seeing familiar faces and before you know it, you will have a whole new circle of friends!

✦

Participate in a fun run or 10K. If you run alongside a man who is jogging at about the same pace as you, it won't be long before the two of you are conversing. Or, if you are not in any shape to be running, you can still compete, just line up near the back with the "fun runners," most of whom will be walking leisurely and enjoying themselves. Come on, you can do it and afterwards you will not only feel good about yourself, but you also will have made several new friends!

✦

Shoot some hoops. Grab a basketball and go to a playground or park and practice your free throws. This is a favorite pastime for many guys and if you are there when a cager arrives, don't be surprised if he asks you to join him in a shoot-around or game of H.O.R.S.E.

✦

Join a co-ed softball team. Contact your local parks and recreation department about leagues. Usually divided into age groups, this allows teams with older players to compete with each other and makes for a more level playing field. Teams practice several times a week and often socialize afterwards. If you can catch a ball . . . you won't want to miss this!

✦ ✦ ✦

Winter Activities

Snow Skiing . . .

Spend the weekend at a ski resort. Even if you don't ski, there are many things you can do during the day. Besides, most of the socializing doesn't begin until the skiers get down from the mountain.

✦

Stay in a lodge that offers their guests many conveniences . . . and then be sure to use them. When choosing a place to stay, consider the following:
- *Whirlpool* – in the evenings you're likely to encounter several fellows easing their sore muscles.
- *Restaurant* – slope bound cuties will be there for breakfast and probably dinner, too.
- *Lounge/entertainment* – music, dancing and men, what else do you need?
- *Fireplace in the lobby* – very conducive for relaxing and chatting with other hotel guests.
- *Game room* – look for a friendly game of Hearts or Gin Rummy to join.

✦

Take ski lessons. Classes on mogul basics will have the most male skiers, but enrolling in any instructional class will get you interacting with other skiers in the group. And, of course, there's always that darling instructor!

✦

Start the day with an early breakfast. Most male skiers like to hit the slopes first thing in the morning, so look for busy breakfast spots about an hour or so before the lifts open. Even if you're not very hungry, be there, if only for a cup of coffee . . . and look your best!

✦

Practice carving your turns. Although there has been a recent surge in young male snowboarders, downhill skiing continues to be popular with the over thirty crowd. **$** Well-to-do bachelors frequent destination resorts (where ski enthusiasts stay a week or more). Two well-known haunts for the rich and famous are Aspen, Colorado, and Deer Valley, Utah. If you have the wherewithal, I suggest you go there . . . you'll be glad you did!

✦

Get in the "single" line at the chairlift . . . and pair up with a handsome guy who is by himself. The longer the ride, the more time you'll have to talk with him. This is a *super* way to meet male skiers and don't be surprised if one of them asks you to meet him for a hot buttered rum at the end of the day!

✦

Hang out at the apres ski lodge . . . even if you aren't skiing. Have lunch in the cafeteria and spend the rest of the afternoon soaking up some sun and watching downhillers on the lower part of the mountain. And don't be shy about visiting with skiers as they return for the day – telling them how good they looked coming down the hill will usually get their attention.

✦

Join a ski club. Members of this active group get together during the winter for numerous weekend outings and vacations to various ski areas. Count on making many new friends, both on the chartered bus you'll take to the resort and at the condo you'll share with several others. During the off season activities abound with bike rides, parties and other member affairs. Many non-skiers participate just for the social enjoyment, so give it a try, I think you'll like this one!

✦

Put on some skinny skis and find a cross country trail. When there is snow on the ground, this is a great alternative to walking or hiking. Locate groomed tracks on golf courses and at cross country facilities or look for popular trails in scenic areas. Be sure to bring plenty of fluids and snacks, you may meet someone who needs a pick-me-up . . . or is it pick-him-up!

✦

Walk along a cross country trail. If you'd rather not ski, you can always walk next to a well-traveled path. And just like busy hiking trails, you never know who may be waiting just beyond the next bend!

✦

Sign up for a day of heli-skiing. This is not for the faint of heart, but if you are an excellent skier, nothing could be finer than powder skiing down virgin mountain slopes with a group of gorgeous men!

✦ ✦ ✦

OTHER WINTER OPTIONS . . .

Spend an afternoon at a ski swap. Lots of fellows attend these events, either to unload older equipment or find something new. Look for shows in the early fall, prior to the first snowfall. Check with local ski shops for more information. Don't miss out . . . you'll be happy you didn't!

✦

Attend the annual ski show in Las Vegas. This is a *really big* exhibition, usually held in the spring and heavily attended by unattached men. If you want to meet a few handsome fellows, this event should not be missed! And be sure to get an invite to one of the vendor parties . . . this may be the opportunity you've been waiting for!

✦

Take a winter driving class. A favorite with the male set is the high-performance course at Bridgestone Winter Driving School in Steamboat Springs, Colorado. Not only will you learn how to handle your car in icy driving conditions, but you may also find more than you can handle in the man department!

✦

Locate a popular snowmobile area. Probably too demanding a sport for most women, but you can still come in contact with many of these hardy males at designated spots where they will be riding these "motorcycles on skis." In addition to equipment rental, there will oftentimes be a snack bar where you can wait for them to finish their laps around the course. And I'll bet it won't be very long before someone offers to take you for a ride!

✦

Go to an ice hockey game. In addition to professional teams, many colleges compete in this fast-paced, aggressive sport. But before you go, find out how it's played. The more knowledgeable you are, the more you will enjoy the game and the easier it will be to converse with those around you. And did I mention . . . you will be surrounded by men?

✦

Watch a broom ball competition . . . frequently enjoyed by guys who are not very experienced or in good enough physical shape to play an actual game of ice hockey. It also is played at a much slower pace and brooms are used instead of sticks to prevent players from getting hurt. Look for friendly contests at ice rinks or other skating areas in the evenings or on weekends. Not only will you giggle a lot, but the boys are awfully cute!

✦ ✦ ✦

SPECTATOR SPORTS

Attend a sporting event. Those with the most potential for meeting sports-minded fellows are football, baseball and basketball. You won't go wrong with any of these, as males are abundant, both as spectators and participants. And don't be afraid to go it alone, people wandering around by themselves are a common sight and most will not even give it a second thought. Besides, once you start talking to those around you, you won't be alone any longer. I've also found, most men think it's great that a woman not only likes sports, but also is confident enough to be there by herself.

✦

Purchase season tickets to professional or college games. You will have the same seat for each game and over the course of several events, you will get to know other season ticket holders around you. If you don't want to invest in a whole season, some venues offer game packages (i.e., 6-game, 24-game). If you buy a couple of smaller ones, for instance, you can sit in several different locations and meet even more men!

✦

Go to the concession stand whenever possible. This is your chance to talk to a fellow standing in line about how the game is going. And it just may lead to something more . . . wilder things have happened!

✦

If you don't have major or minor league sports in your community . . . look for local college and high school games. You will be surprised at the number of adults who attend these events, especially when it's the only game in town. Take football, for example, in some parts of the country, high school games can draw more than 20,000 fans. Plus, you never know who you might bump into . . . I recently read that actor, Kevin Costner occasionally attends baseball games at his college alma mater where he once played on the varsity squad. Give it a try and see who you meet!

✦

See what's going on at a nearby park. If you don't spend much time at parks and other local recreational areas, you're missing out on numerous opportunities to meet many unattached fellows. Activities and participants are constantly changing and if a men's sporting event is being played, there will be plenty of them around. Not only do the boys like to participate, but they also enjoy watching their friends play. So, head over right now . . . there's a good chance you'll meet someone while you're there.

✦

Enjoy an evening men's softball game. Look for the 30+, 40+ and senior leagues. Do I need to remind you . . . nine guys per team + male spectators = several dozen guys!

✦

Observe a basketball half-court or one-on-one tournament. These are often depicted on television beer commercials and are extremely popular with "b-ball" players of all ages. In addition to organized competitions, look for friendly games at parks, school grounds and gymnasiums.

✦

Do not miss a chance to watch a Rugby match. Believe it or not, many of these crazy fellows who play this English form of football (but without pads and helmets) are attorneys. After the game most of the players usually go to a sports bar or tavern to celebrate. Once you know where that is . . . be ready to party!

✦

Watch a track meet . . . particularly at the college and high school level. If you watched the Olympics, you know how entertaining this will be . . . but even better, is how many men there will be!

✦

Take in a boxing match. You'll find lots of fellows at this predominately male venue. Many gambling houses also present boxing entertainment and after the bout, the casino will be packed with fight spectators. Although opportunities abound at gaming establishments, it will be even better on these nights!

✦

Holler at the bad guy at a wrestling match. Extremely popular with the male species – why, I do not understand, but if you attend one of these matches there will be plenty of men to choose from. Another alternative is collegiate wrestling, where the matches are legit. The crowds will be smaller, but most spectators will be male.

✦

Sit with a group of fellows at roller derby. Not available everywhere, but like wrestling and boxing, many men get a kick out of watching this staged performance.

✦

Attend an Over the Line tournament . . . which is popular in beach communities of California. Hundreds of three-man teams compete for fun and prizes, plus there are tens of thousands of spectators. One of the largest is sponsored by OMBAC (Old

Mission Beach Athletic Club) in San Diego. You won't want to miss this, especially if you are partial to suntanned men with muscular bodies!

◆

$ Go to a polo match. This darling of the rich and famous has gained notoriety from Prince Charles and the movie *Pretty Woman*. Here's your chance to dress up, put on the charm and meet a few civilized gentlemen.

◆

Cheer for the bull riders and calf ropers at a rodeo. There will be cow***boys*** everywhere . . . and the only effort required on your part is to just show up!

◆ ◆ ◆

BOATING AND WATER SPORTS

THE WATERFRONT . . .

Spend the day near a boat launch. There will be a constant stream of boaters waiting to get in or out of the water and you'll have many opportunities to meet some of them. And if all goes well, someone may ask you to come along . . . hey, it could happen!

◆

Walk around the boat docks. Mornings, late afternoons, or early evenings will be active with boaters and fishermen readying their boats or returning from the day's activity. Not only that, but sailing and cruising vessels take a lot of maintenance and, consequently, their owners spend many hours each week working on them. The more time you can stay in the area increases your chances of meeting one of them. But be prepared and pack some extra gear, as you just never know where a casual conversation may lead. And, of course, you want to be ready when someone asks you to join him for a day on his cabin cruiser! **$** And while you are wandering around, look for large yachts – the bigger the boat, the more money it takes to both purchase and maintain it. And I almost forgot . . . many single fellows also live-a-board their sailboats.

So, if you see a fellow in the area with a towel and dopp kit, there's a good chance he's unattached and his boat is nearby.

✦

Be around the docks before or after sailing regattas. Most of the crews will be milling around prior to and following the race. Contact yacht clubs and other sailing groups to find out when these events will be held – usually in the evenings during the week and, of course, on the weekends.

✦

Get to the marina in the early a.m. and have breakfast at a nearby café. Boaters like to get an early start and the chances are very good they'll stop for something to eat first.

✦

Frequent businesses near marinas and waterfront areas. Yachtsmen are likely to patronize these establishments when they're not out on the water. Restaurants and bars will also be very busy after racing events when crews are celebrating or commiserating. Once you go there, you'll see what I mean!

✦

Put together a breakfast picnic and watch the sunrise from the end of a dock. Pack fresh fruit, croissants and a large thermos of hot coffee. Bring along a couple of extra mugs and offer an early morning riser a cup of java. But don't be surprised if he's so grateful, he invites you out on his boat!

✦ ✦ ✦

BOATS . . .

Learn to trim a jib . . . and become part of the sailing world where participants are predominately male. Take a class in fundamentals, so you'll be prepared to help out when that gentleman you're soon to meet invites you for a cruise!

✦

Be part of a sailboat race. Skippers are continually looking for crewmembers and once you know some sailing basics, offer your services. Then after the race you can participate in the victory celebration and meet several of the fellows who competed on other sailboats. You'll find that this is a close-knit group where everyone knows everybody else, so once you meet one, you'll meet the rest of them!

✦

Take a navigation class. You will probably be the only woman. If you like these odds, get yourself enrolled pronto!

✦

Sign up for a boating safety or maintenance class. The U.S. Coast Guard and other marine groups offer classes for the novice, including boating skills and seamanship. In addition to the males in your class, the instructors will be Coast Guard sea*men*!

✦

Offer to cook for a long sailboat race. If you have the free time and the desire to be on a yacht for several days with a group of men, this is the ideal situation for you!

✦

Shop for a used boat. You will find many water vessels for sale at marinas and in showrooms, but you can also answer ads in the newspaper. As with classic automobiles, you won't find many women selling boats, so here's your chance to meet an outdoors fellow and talk with him face-to-face. Again, be prepared, as you should have some knowledge about the type of boat before spending a couple of hours with the owner. **$** And, of course, the larger the yacht, the more money he has.

✦

Buy a small daysailer and participate in a racing program. You will meet lots of sailing enthusiasts and the initial investment will not cost you an arm and a leg. Check with local clubs to find out the most popular classes of boats that are being raced and then purchase one of them and start competing in regattas.

✦

Go to a boat show. In the spring before the boating season begins, look for large exhibitions at convention centers and smaller "in-the-water" shows. Fellow boaters attend these events in large numbers and you will meet lots of yachtsmen . . . believe me!

✦

$ Meet men at a yacht club. This is a fabulous way to meet gentlemen of all ages. You don't need a boat, but you should have a love of or desire to have one some day. In addition to boating activities, clubs offer dining and full-service bars . . . plus, there will always be someone around to talk to!

✦

Seek a part-time job with a charter company. In addition to pleasure boat charters, many individuals rent yachts for private parties and help is often needed with food preparation, crew and hostessing. By the way, many male guests attend these functions and this is a great way to meet them.

✦

Paddle a kayak. This fast-growing sport is becoming very popular with outdoorsmen. Once thought of as a dangerous activity, its new popularity is with those who are looking for a more laid-back experience on peaceful lakes and rivers. You can rent equipment and receive instruction at many outdoor stores, marinas and kayak schools. This is one sport almost anyone can do, so why not you?

✦ ✦ ✦

WATER ACTIVITIES . . .

Spend time at a water ski area. You don't necessarily have to ski, as there will be many individuals on the shoreline enjoying the sun and water. Most skiers stay in local campgrounds, so pick out a campsite near a group of guys and once the socializing begins, get ready for a good time!

✦

Swim at an athletic club. The noon hour and after the workday are the best times to be around male swimmers. Although many females are interested in water aerobics classes, very few enjoy the more grueling distance swimming. And don't worry about how you look, after doing this for a few months, you'll be a knockout!

✦

Observe a surfing contest. Even though the majority of surfboarders are youngsters, you will still find many old-timers out in the water "walking the nose" or on the beach watching the big wave riders.

✦

Take in a water polo match. Not the most well-attended spectator sport, but it is exciting to watch and played by men with incredible physiques! Very similar to hockey or soccer – one team tries to get the ball into the opposing team's net. Look for matches at colleges and high schools that have a strong swim program.

✦

Learn to scuba dive . . . a popular sport for underwater enthusiasts, and, as you know by now, the fellows will outnumber the ladies. Instructional costs include all gear and equipment, plus certification at the end of the class. Give this a try and it won't be long before you'll be part of a buddy system!

✦ ✦ ✦

FISHING

Go fishing. I know some of you may be going "yuk!" But ladies, we're talking lots of men! For those of you willing to give this a try, you will be well rewarded. The very best time to go is on "opening day" (the first day of fishing season). Read the local fishing column in the sports page to find out where popular areas are located, as this is where you'll want to be. If nothing else, at least go and watch them. Really! Take a picnic basket and enjoy a nice day in the out-of-doors . . . you will be glad you did!

✦

Hook a marlin on a pleasure fishing trip. Very popular are deep sea and sport fishing charters. Be prepared to set out in the early a.m. and by the time you get back, you will have enough fish and new friends for quite a party!

✦

Cut a hole in the ice and catch a bass. In some northern climates where lakes freeze over in the winter, you will see hundreds of men fishing, especially on the weekends. If you'd rather not sit around with a frozen tush, try doing something else that will put you around them, like selling snacks, cups of hot coffee or cocoa.

✦

Sign up for a fishing excursion . . . and spend the day with a group of anglers. Many outfitters offer fishing tours and, for a fee, will take you to their "secret" spots. During summer months you may find many families on these adventures, in which case, ask to be placed with an adult group or sign up for a spring or fall trip when participants are primarily males. With any kind of luck you'll catch a big one . . . and I don't mean a mackerel!

✦

Stay in a cabin at the edge of a popular river. Sit outside and watch the floaters go by. And don't be shy about inviting a couple of them over for a drink after they're finished for the day . . . they'll be more than happy to tell you about the one that got away!

✦

Cast a line from the end of a dock. Lots of men enjoy this kind of fishing. Plus, it is a good way to spend an early morning, even if all you do is walk around the pier and talk with other people who are wandering about.

✦

Rent a boat and try your luck. Go to a nearby lake with good fishing and get a motorboat for a half-day. The main hub of activity will be at the marina where you will rent the skiff, which means this is where most of the men will be. If nothing else, hang around for awhile and talk with returning anglers and find out if they've caught anything . . . you could be lucky, too, and catch your limit!

✦

Wet a line in a stream and give fly fishing a try. *Extremely* popular with men and is a beautiful, peaceful sport – remember the scenes in *A River Runs Through It*? And if you take lessons, you will be the only gal in the class. Once you learn the basic techniques, go to a large open area (such as a football field) and practice your "10 o'clock to 2 o'clock" casts. You won't be there long before someone comes over and asks what you're doing. But the best part comes later when you find a popular fly fishing stream . . . and it's just you, the elements and a lot of men!

◆

Learn to tie flies. These are the life-like insects used as bait and many avid fisherman make their own. Again, you will more than likely be the only woman in the class . . . if you don't believe me, give it a try!

◆

Become a member of an angling club. Not only are these groups predominately male, but they also meet regularly and go on many excursions together. During the fishing season, you will never again want for something to do on a Saturday!

◆ ◆ ◆

THE OUTDOOR SPORTSMAN

Spend a weekend in a popular outdoor area. Locales that are well known for activities, like hunting, fishing and mountaineering should be your first choice. If you want to find lots of fellows, this is where you should be looking. During their respective seasons, these areas will be crowded with nothing but outdoorsmen . . . and, of course, you will want to be there to take advantage of this surplus of eligible men! Browse through sporting and outdoor magazines . . . like *Sports Afield* and *Outdoor Life* and look for advertisements of places to go. By the way, it is no coincidence that those who participate in outdoor activities are called sports*men* and outdoors*men*!

◆

Head out on a backcountry trip. There are many adventures offered by outfitters to isolated areas and are extremely popular with outdoorsmen. If you feel adventuresome and are willing to put up with a few inconveniences . . . you will be well rewarded!

◆

Find a camping site . . . near a group of guys. Many families enjoy this activity, but there will also be lots of single fellows, especially if there's good fishing or boating nearby. You will get to know your camp mates fairly quickly, so be sure to bring extra snacks and some good music . . . and be ready for a swell time! Plus, while preparing for your trip, you will have a chance to meet other male enthusiasts, as you spend time in backpacking and outdoor stores picking up camping essentials.

✦

Go to a national park for the day. Federally maintained areas are filled during summer months with vacationers and dayhikers enjoying the trails and scenery. The more experienced hikers will be on rugged backcountry trails. Even if you are not in very good shape, hike as far as you can and see who you meet along the way!

✦

Be active in the Sierra Club. There are thousands of chapters throughout the country and most are extremely active, sponsoring dozens of activities every month. Look into this environmentally friendly group . . . there's lots of potential!

✦

Fill a knapsack with goodies and set out on a trek. This is an extremely popular activity in many parts of the country with people of all ages and degrees of physical fitness enjoying the great outdoors. Look for popular hiking trails in the woods or mountains and along rivers or lakes. You will find that hikers are a very friendly bunch, so enjoy the scenery and the chance meetings along the way. And as a precaution, always be sure to let someone know where you're going and when you expect to get back.

✦

Locate areas that are popular with off-roaders. Interest is widespread with men who have ATV's, dirt bikes, dune buggies and other four-wheel drives. And, as far as lodging is concerned, either stay at a nearby inn or locate a campground in the area, which is where many of them will be. Look for rugged trails to explore at many state and national forests. For information and maps, contact the U.S. Forest Service office nearest you.

✦

For a fun outdoor adventure, try white-water rafting . . . and meet other thrillseekers. It doesn't matter if you go with a friend or not, as you will be placed in a raft with several other adventuresome folks. Trips can last anywhere from a half-day to several weeks, but the longer and more dangerous the trip, the more men. The granddaddy of them all is the Grand Canyon and is a thrilling, extremely challenging experience that can't be beat. I guarantee you will cherish the experience and the people you meet! If you have the time, I highly recommend doing this one.

✦

Take aim at a target range . . . both shooting ranges and gun clubs are great for finding men. If you are afraid of firearms or don't know how to use one, take a beginning class. Some facilities also have dining and lounge areas where you can relax and observe the numerous marksmen.

✦

Go to a sporting clays competition. This is immensely popular with men of all ages and is one of the fastest growing sports in America with more than three million participants per year in both competition and fellowship. Courses offer shooters a variety of distances, angles and target sizes and all levels of ability can compete. You do not want to miss any of these events!

✦

Try your luck at a trap and skeet range . . . which are frequented by male sharpshooters and very popular with hunters and rifle owners. There are several organizations you can contact for events in your locale. Why not go and see how easy it is to meet some of these fellows!

✦

Get involved in Ducks Unlimited. One of the largest privately funded conservation organizations in the U.S. and its primary emphasis is with wetlands conservation and waterfowl hunting. The membership is comprised mainly of men, so find a local meeting . . . and go!

✦

Picnic near a climbing area. This is a neat way to meet guys, as the place will be crawling with them (no pun intended). Check with outdoor stores for nearby climbing sites and then join other spectators as you watch them scale those granite faces.

✦

Enroll in a climbing school. Again, this is an activity where male participation is dominant. And now, you can even climb indoors at some sports clubs and retail stores that have newly installed climbing walls. By the way, this is a fantastic way to get in shape and is much easier to do than you might imagine.

✦ ✦ ✦

10

WHERE THEY SHOP

I know of a singer who wanted to meet someone who shared her love for music. Consequently, she spent most of her free time at stereo and music stores, talking with customers and salesmen who came into the shops. Not only did this resourceful woman figure out the best places to meet music lovers, but she also kept at it until she eventually found the man she was looking for; and shortly after they moved in together, she became the lead singer in his band.

This gal was fortunate. Her passion was in an area where males are prevalent. Even if you are not so lucky, there are many opportunities where you, too, can meet men in retail establishments, particularly where they are the primary shoppers. For instance, if you needed a warm, heavy sweater, you would probably go to a department store. Instead, why not look in an outdoors store or a ski shop where the chances of bumping into a man is more likely.

Although men probably hate shopping more than anything else and will put off doing it until the last minute, when they do hit the stores it will usually be late in the day or first thing on weekend mornings.

The following suggestions will give you a few shopping alternatives you may not have thought of. And to ensure that your efforts are not wasted in an empty shop, wait for someone interesting to enter before going in, especially if it's a small store. And, of course, feel free to talk with those around you . . . and smile!

BUILDING SUPPLIES

Frequent a home center or hardware store. Even though women are patronizing home improvement centers more than in the past, men are still the main consumers of tools and lumber. Notice which articles you can buy here instead of the grocery store, such as trash bags and batteries. This should be your main source for many household and garden supplies – include at least one visit to a hardware store as part of your weekly shopping routine.

✦

Visit a lumber yard. This is not as consumer-oriented as home centers, but loaded with building contractors, especially in the mornings. And, of course, feel free to ask fellow shoppers about items which you are unfamiliar. While there look for some shelving or decorative molding for a new look in your bedroom. Maybe one of these guys will offer to give you some help.

✦

Browse through a woodworking store. These specialize in exotic woods and tools for the craftsman . . . and there won't be another woman within sight! While you're there, pick out a few basic items for a home repair kit.

✦

Wander through an architectural salvage yard . . . and meet one of many building contractors and architects who use this as a source for old and unusual accents in client landscapes and interiors. There are many hidden treasures, so look around for something to screen an unsightly view or for a vine to wrap around.

✦ ✦ ✦

OUTDOORS AND SPORTING GOODS

Wander around a sporting goods emporium . . . and find a warm jacket or new pair of walking shoes to wear. Also, this is a good source for information on different sporting groups and activities.

✦

Find something new to wear at a golf outlet. In addition to golfing equipment, retail centers offer a wide-range of clothing and accessories for men and women. And with any kind of luck, you just might find something you like . . . and I don't mean a cute shirt!

✦

Browse through a ski outlet. The best time to visit is in the fall, when skiers start thinking of snow on the slopes. While you're there, look for a new parka or sweater to take on your next alpine vacation.

✦

Try out a 10-speed at a bicycle stop. Very popular with male cyclists, especially stores that specialize in top-of-the-line bikes. Check out the clothing and accessories, not to mention all the men in those tight little shorts!

✦

Locate a shop catering to anglers. During fishing season, you'll find lots of men replenishing their tackle boxes and checking out the newest gear. Also, find a store that specializes in fly fishing . . . this is one place you don't want to overlook!

✦

Spend time in a backpacking store. Outdoor enthusiasts have a lot of paraphernalia which they purchase from these outlets. Even if you're not a fan of outdoor activities, you can still patronize these places and find items for your own use, like active sportswear, good rain gear, items for your home emergency kit and lots of gift ideas. Also, don't forget about Army/Navy surplus stores, they sell a variety of outdoor gear and camping equipment, so the clientele will be similar. And if someone catches your eye, engage him in a conversation . . . it may turn out, he's had his eye on you, too!

✦

Go to a gun show. Although many women are uncomfortable with firearms, if you want to be where the men are . . . this is the place! Just go and browse around, you'll be surrounded by more gun collectors than you can imagine!

✦ ✦ ✦

HIGH-QUALITY STUFF

Find a new piece of software for your PC. The vast majority of computer store patrons are male and you can spend the better part of an afternoon playing with the latest technology or trying out new software applications. If you haven't been in one of these places lately. . . you may be missing out on a great opportunity. By the way, did I mention, this is where I met my husband. You see, it does happen!

✦

$ Listen to a sound system at an electronics outlet. Men love good stereos and big-screen televisions. On weekends high-end audio/video stores *are filled* with male audiophiles. You can listen to music in one of the display rooms and compare speakers or ask someone why he prefers one particular system over another. The longer you stick around, the more potential of meeting an interesting fellow.

✦

$ Browse through an art gallery. These shops are usually clumped together in certain areas of the city and you can easily spend several hours going from gallery to gallery. Not only will this put you in a position to meet well-off gentlemen who have an eye for art, but with any kind of luck, one of them will have his eye on you!

✦

$ Spend the day looking at expensive automobiles . . . particularly dealerships specializing in high-performance autos and old classics. Greatly prized by men of means, there will always be some handsome fellow admiring one of these beauties. And don't be concerned about salesmen pressuring you, they are less aggressive than those selling lesser-priced automobiles and will leave you alone, if requested.

✦

$ Check out cognacs at a liquor store. Men of means are partial to sipping on high-quality brandies and liqueurs. While there, pick up an expensive bottle of Courvoisier for that wealthy gentleman you're soon to meet!

✦

$ Select a nice bottle of Merlot from a wine merchant. Men are the main consumers of fine wines and champagnes and the more time you spend in these stores becoming familiar with Montrachet and Bordeaux vintners, the greater your chances of meeting male connoisseurs.

✦

$ Pretend you have money and go to the most expensive stores . . . try on shoes, clothing, jewelry and furs. If you see a potential "sighting," don't pass up an occasion to strike up a conversation. But be sure to dress as though you can afford to buy whatever it is you are looking at!

✦ ✦ ✦

NOSTALGIA

Visit a coin shop . . . where the main patrons are male. Almost every man had a coin collection when he was young and many have continued their collecting. While there ask when the next local coin show will be held . . . you won't want to miss it!

✦

Sell your vinyl oldies. If you have some albums you'd like to get rid of, here's a way to meet music lovers. Depending on the record type – rock, jazz, or classical – you will be contacted by many fellows who want to add to their collections.

✦

Pick out an old favorite at a used record shop. Most purchasers of old LPs are males and when you see a potential prospect, browse through a stack of records next to him. Ask what he's searching for and offer to keep an eye out while you look through your section. Who knows, you may find an old classic he'd like to come over and listen to!

✦

Spend the day looking for male memorabilia . . . like war mementos and sports souvenirs. Be around nostalgia seekers as you browse through shops that sell these collectibles. And if you've got something they want . . . you can be sure they'll be contacting you!

✦

Trade in some old books. Rare and used book sales are popular with male collectors, particularly those featuring history, science fiction, mystery and western folklore titles. If you have a fondness for old novels, you should definitely attend.

✦ ✦ ✦

OTHER SHOPPING OPPORTUNITIES

$ Patronize men's clothing stores . . . and look for a cotton shirt to wear with your leggings. The more expensive the store, the greater the probability of meeting a man of means. If you see a gentleman by himself, he is probably a bachelor, as most wives purchase their husband's clothes. (The exception is suits, which, of course, need fitting before they can be tailored.) Get his attention by asking, "You're about the same size as my brother, would this fit you?"

✦

Try on a cowboy hat at a Western emporium . . . and ask a gent nearby how it looks.

✦

Check out leather jackets at a motorcycle outlet. No longer just a place for biker gangs to hang out, these shops are springing up all over the country and offering more than high-horsepowered "Harley hogs." Many well-to-do men are getting into the sport, as evidenced in recent articles about the rich and famous and their ultimate motorcycle getaways. If you've not been in one of these shops, you'll be quite surprised with what you'll find!

✦

Browse for jewelry in a pawn shop. Women rarely patronize these secondhand shops and not all are sleazy. Look for ones in nice areas of town that specialize in watches, musical instruments, tools, televisions and stereos, which are the items most men will be looking for.

✦

Peruse CD titles at a music store. Many fellows will be picking out titles in the jazz and classical sections, as well as browsing through blues and rock music. Ask someone nearby what he'd recommend for lazy afternoon listening.

✦

Purchase a chess set at an adult game store. Males are the primary shoppers when it comes to board games. This, also, is a good place to get info on local chess tournaments, clubs and other related activities.

✦

$ Admire the workmanship of handmade furniture. Any man with an appreciation for fine craftsmanship will be nearby, especially with the resurgence of the more masculine lines of furniture from the Arts and Crafts era.

✦

$ Familiarize yourself with a marine hardware store. This is where boat owners shop for gear and also is a good source for gifts with a nautical theme. Don't overlook ship chandelries that cater to wealthy yachtsmen, as they, too, have excellent potential. Be sure to check these places out and don't be surprised at where a casual conversation may lead!

✦

Pick up some carnuba wax at an auto parts store. There's lots more here to shop for than automobile paraphernalia. In addition to plenty of men, there are things like upholstery cleaners, air fresheners and flashlights.

◆

Become familiar with feed supplies, tack shops, or farm equipment centers. In rural and agricultural areas, this is where you'll find ranchers and farmers purchasing needed items.

◆

Rent a space and sell something at a swap meet. Not only will you have a great time, you will meet lots of people. Ask friends for any articles they'd like you to sell for them – the more good stuff you have, the greater number of folks who will stop to browse. If you have any free time after your wares have been sold, wander around and look for items that attract men, like auto parts, sporting equipment and other "guy stuff." Not only will you find most of the fellows there, but you may come away with more than you bargained for!

◆

Don't miss large retail clearance sales . . . particularly those men will be interested in, such as car stereos, musical instruments, sporting and camping equipment. Once you see who's there, you'll know why this has been suggested!

◆

Make a bid at an auction. Contact auctioneers about coming sales. Many liquidators not only hold regularly scheduled vendues on their premises, but also at outside locations where they preside over special sales. Any of the following auctions will yield an abundance of men:
- **$** *Fine art and antiques*
- **$** *Estate sales*
- **$** *Expensive and vintage automobiles*
- **$** *Real estate*
- *Business equipment and furniture*
- *Repossessed automobiles and boats*
- *Government surplus*
- *Tools, machinery and farm equipment*

◆

Participate in a police auction. Find out when upcoming liquidations of confiscated and unclaimed items will be held. Male attendees will be bidding on everything from cars and boats to bicycles and jewelry. If you've never gone to one, you'll be pleased at what you'll find . . . and I don't mean auction items!

✦ ✦ ✦

11

WHERE THEY TRAVEL

Every day hundreds of thousands of travelers go through our major airports and the largest segment of those traveling during the week are businessmen. This means meeting single men while you're away from home should be relatively easy. Here are a few ideas for your next vacation or weekend getaway that will put you in contact with males who are away from home.

TRANSPORTATION

Fly whenever you can. There are so many opportunities to meet men when traveling on an airplane. Stories abound with individuals becoming romantically involved with someone they've met while in the air . . . it can happen to you, too!

✦

Book your flights during the week . . . when business trips are usually taken. If you are traveling over the weekend, increase your odds of being around businessmen and leave on Friday evening and return Monday morning.

✦

$ Sit in business or first class. This is where most well-to-do passengers and executives are seated. If you can afford the added cost, it could be money well spent.

✦

Sit in an aisle seat whenever possible. This not only gives you a chance to talk with your seatmate, but also the fellow on the opposite side of the aisle. Other good locations are center seating (when more than two seats, then you have someone on both sides of you) and seats in the back near the restrooms. The latter may be bumpier and noisier, but it gives you a chance to visit with passengers while they wait for the facilities.

✦

Take a shuttle to the airport. This is a great way to meet businessmen and other airline passengers who use this service . . . so take advantage of it!

✦

Get to the airport several hours before your flight is scheduled to leave . . . and use this time to talk with people who are waiting in the terminal. If you see a man by himself, just plop yourself next to him and ask where he's going. I can't tell you how many interesting gentlemen I've met this way!

✦

$ Wait for your flight in an airline's private lounge. Most major airline hubs have well-appointed facilities for the exclusive use of their club members. Serving food and beverages in a relaxed setting, they are very popular with frequent flyers, particularly businessmen and well-to-do gentlemen. The investment is well worth it, especially if you travel often. Check with individual airlines for membership information.

✦

Get a shoeshine at the airport. While waiting for your flight, sit next to a man getting his shoes spiffed up and have your leather pumps done, too. This usually takes no more than 5 - 10 minutes, so talk fast, otherwise he will be gone before you know it!

✦

Commuters are a great way to meet men . . . as you can chat with many different passengers during the trip. Instead of being in the first group to board, wait a bit so you can pick out who you want to sit next to, rather than the other way around.

◆

Take an overnight train trip. If you haven't tried a short jaunt on the local Amtrak, you're missing a great opportunity. You will have many occasions to visit with travelers, in addition to talking with seatmates, you can spend time in the club or observation car while chatting with other passengers. A favorite overnight trip in the winter is to a ski resort in a neighboring state. All I can say is party, party, party!

◆

When eating in the dining car, ask to be seated with a male passenger. Mealtime gives you another chance to get to know other travelers who are by themselves. And if all goes well, you may be spending a lot more time together!

◆ ◆ ◆

LODGING

Although this section is geared to places to stay when traveling, you can also apply the following suggestions to hotels in your locale. There is no rule that says you have to be on the road to meet men from out-of-town.

Stay in hotels with lots of amenities. The more things to do, the more chances to interact with different people, and the better your odds of encountering someone of interest. But there is one catch, you will have to leave your room if you want to meet anyone!

◆

Look for accommodations near airports and business districts. Businessmen like to be close to their meeting location or near the airport, especially if they are arriving late or departing early in the day. Lodging near shopping malls are also very good, as male travelers prefer doing more than sitting in their rooms at night. The more activities in the evening, the more desirable that hotel will be to them. And don't miss breakfast in the morning . . . I don't need to tell you who will be there!

✦

$ Obtain a room at a high-end hotel. The more expensive the inn, the more wealthy the clientele. If you can't afford to stay the night, at least spend some time there. Remember, you don't have to be a guest to enjoy the amenities. Also, many top-notch hotels are part of resorts that offer golf, tennis and other activities. The more sports options, the more men you'll meet.

✦

When traveling on business, stay in a hotel instead of a motel . . . even if it means using some of your own money. Hotels are much more conducive for meeting individuals roaming around the lobby or using other facilities within the complex, than places where lodgers stay in their rooms and watch television.

✦

Frequent hotel restaurants and lounges. This is a good way to meet guests, even if you are not staying in the hotel. Those with meeting facilities also have potential. Not only will conference goers stay where the meeting is being held, but they will often stick around and do something in the evenings.

✦

Have your hair done at a salon in a nice hotel. Afterwards spend a few hours in one of the restaurants or lounges. Here's your chance to meet someone when you're feeling good about yourself . . . and looking good, too!

✦

$ Travel to resorts and destinations that cater to the rich and famous. Put yourself around the well-heeled and you'll have a much greater potential of reeling in a big one!

✦

Look for lodging that offers complimentary breakfasts . . . and mingle with early-rising businessmen. They really like these places, as it's one less meal out of their per diem.

✦ ✦ ✦

WEEKEND GETAWAYS

Get involved with an adventure group. The more activities planned that men enjoy doing, the more likely they will participate. If you are unable to find an existing group, remember you can start your own. This would be a good candidate, especially if you plan weekend getaways, like river rafting, hiking, or campouts.

✦

Drive as far as a tank of gas will take you. For example, if you get 300 miles per fill-up, then measure half that distance (you have to get back) and draw a circle with a radius of 150 miles. Pick a spot within the circle and go there for the weekend. A change in scenery may be all it takes!

✦

Hop on a plane or train and go somewhere . . . for a day or two. With any kind of luck you will meet someone on the way who can show you the sights or at least tell you which places not to miss. So, give it a chance, you've got nothing to lose!

✦

Roll up all the change you've been saving and get away. Anything that gets you out of the house is a good thing. As you know by now, you're not going to meet anyone if you're sitting at home watching television!

✦

Offer to housesit or trade homes with a friend in another city. Not only a nice getaway and change of pace, but now you're free to put the *POP* to work and make some new friends. Then the next time you visit, you'll have several contacts and they in turn will introduce you to many of their friends . . . and you know where it can go from there!

✦

Rent a waterfront cabin for the weekend in a popular area . . . and be where there's a lot of activity. Take a walk along the shoreline, ride a bike around, or sit on your deck and visit with passers-by. Your goal . . . meet as many new people as possible.

✦

Visit a nearby town. Do some shopping, dine alfresco near a busy activity area, or visit other points of interest. Also, be sure to pick up a schedule of events from the Chamber of Commerce and if something is going on while you're there, don't miss it. Remember, the more outdoor recreational attractions, the more men you'll see. Don't just sit there and think about it . . . go do it!

✦

Take a weekend cruise. Singles cruises are very popular on the two coasts and the shorter jaunts will have lots of men aboard. And for those of you uncomfortable going alone, ask the cruise line to pair you up with another single woman. If you feel like getting away, this just may be what the doctor ordered!

✦

Go to a neighboring attraction . . . like a lake, sporting event, or other activity of male interest. And make sure it's far enough away that you'll have to spend the night. Then the next morning go out for breakfast . . . and smile. Believe it or not, if you do this enough, it won't be long before you start making many new friendships. Besides, what else are you doing?

✦ ✦ ✦

DESTINATION IDEAS

Sign up for a vacation for singles. The destination will usually determine the ratio of unattached males to females, but your travel planner should have some notion of which ones will have a larger concentration of men. Also, go online – there are a myriad of travel opportunities for singles on the Net. Pick one out and go for it!

✦

Add an extra day at one end or the other of your trip. Now you have additional time to meet even more individuals, so use this opportunity to explore the area, visit with friends and make several new contacts.

✦

Relax for the weekend at a wilderness lodge. These establishments cater to hunters, fishermen and backcountry sportsmen. And since most women are not into these activities, the best way to meet these outdoorsmen is to spend time where they will be staying. While the boys are out in the wilderness, you can walk around and enjoy the beauty of the area and then when they get back, you'll be waiting to reap the rewards. By the way, hunting lodges on opening day will be filled to capacity. Go ahead and make a reservation . . . you'll be glad you did!

✦

Ask a friend or colleague for a contact at your destination . . . male, of course! Get in touch with him prior to your arrival date and see if he would like to join you for dinner. If he has the time, ask him to show you a few of the sights and some local haunts. But the best part, is not only will you have a new friend who lives in the area, but he may turn out to be a keeper!

✦

Find a car museum that is close to a gambling spot. Harrah's Automotive Museum in Reno, Nevada, is a great guy getaway – gambling and old autos . . . any man's dream if I ever did see!

✦

Participate in a travel group . . . and get involved with other individuals for frequent weekend getaways and extended vacations. If you are forming a group, have in mind the first trip's destination to assure men will want to join. Then advertise, for example: "Travel group forming for singles over 40, first trip is a golf vacation in Hawaii, future trips include kayaking through the San Juans and hiking in Tibet."

✦

Take a bicycle trip overseas. Wine country tours and other European destinations are very popular with cyclists. If you enjoy two-wheeling, here is an enjoyable way to see the sights and meet other bicycling enthusiasts. Check with your travel agent, local bicycle clubs, or go online for upcoming excursions.

✦

Attend a sports camp. There are many packages available offering expert instruction and accommodations for tennis, running and many other sports. Buy a specialty magazine for the activity which you are interested and check the display ads for clinics or camps. And, of course, you can always go online where there is a great deal of information. For those who are not sports-minded, make a reservation separate from the instruction package. Most of these resorts are located in warm weather areas of the country and there will be many other activities for you to enjoy.

✦

Spend a week at spring training. This means going to Arizona or Florida and watching baseball. It is a relaxed atmosphere for both players and fans and if you want to meet one of the single ballplayers . . . this is the place to be!

✦

$ Sign up for a fantasy baseball camp. Many men with a secret desire to know what it is like to be a professional ballplayer will go through this mini-training camp. It's not cheap, so most of these pro-ball wannabes are well-off individuals.

✦

$ Reserve space on a European Formula 1 tour. This is the granddaddy of all automobile racing and is the most popular motorsport event in Europe, stopping in 16 different countries during the racing season. Probably the most well-known is the Monaco Grand Prix in May with its attraction of the rich and famous. Closer to home is the Canadian Grand Prix in Montreal during June and coming in 2000 the return of F1 racing to the Indianapolis Speedway. Contact your travel agent or Grand Prix Tours, 888-RACES-F1 for more information. Oh, and did I mention . . . you will be surrounded by lots of eligible men!

✦

Plan a golf vacation. If you play a fairly consistent game of golf, this is a great holiday. Chose a destination and stop along the way at different cities, playing at a new course every day or two. Call ahead for tee times and ask to be paired with male threesomes. Not only will you have an enjoyable trip, but you may end up staying a little longer than you planned!

✦

$ Vacation at a golf school. Many weekend golfers and serious players participate in these learning experiences. Located at destination resorts around the country, they are usually sold as complete packages, offering professional golf instruction, greens fees and lodging. Check with your local course pro or golf magazines for schools and their locations.

✦

Set sail on a cruise for singles. There are several outfits in the Caribbean that offer hands-on sailing adventures for small groups of unmarried individuals. By the end of the cruise, not only will you be proficient at handling a yacht, but you will have cultivated several new friendships . . . anyone of which could last a lifetime!

✦

Invest in a timeshare . . . at a popular destination area. Anywhere there are water activities, ski resorts, or golf communities will have lots of men. Some are more popular with singles than others, so check them out before committing yourself to an investment of this kind.

✦

Go to Mexico. This is a mecca for unattached males. Just about any beach or fishing community will be swarming with guys. This is one destination that should become an annual event, if not more often!

✦

Visit communities that are jumping off points for wilderness areas. Many sportsmen enjoy rugged, backcountry environments and the more outdoor activities available, the better they like it. Look for areas noted for male favorites, like hiking, climbing, camping and fishing, as the area will be teeming with men. Not only will you find a large number of them living in the vicinity, but also vacationing there.

✦

Get involved in ecotourism. This is for those who are interested in the exploration of the wildlife, cultural and environmental aspects of a specific locale. According to the Ecotourism Society, of the 528 million who have taken an ecotrip in recent years, 15% go it alone. The average ages are 35-54 and the most popular destinations are to Central America, particularly Costa Rica. For more information check with a travel agent or outfitter who is certified to provide this specific type of travel.

✦

Embark on an exotic adventure. Try something off the beaten path, such as scuba diving in the Galapagos Islands, exploring the Amazon, or experiencing the spirituality of Machu Pichu in the Andes. Your level of physical fitness should determine the difficulty of the trip, however, the more rigorous and demanding, the greater the likelihood of encountering an adventuresome male. There are more than 8,000 outfitters offering a variety of adventure vacations, plus you'll find several books, magazines and numerous websites that feature great outdoor treks.

✦

$ Join a group on safari. Very few women go on these excursions especially if it is big game hunting (which, by the way, only wealthy hunters participant in). There also are photographing safaris where you visit villages and spend time with the natives in their primitive culture. Either way, you will definitely have to rough it. If you can afford it, you will more than likely be the only woman among several men . . . and you can't beat those odds!

✦

If you don't want to travel alone . . . get a guide to show you the sights, especially in foreign countries. Check with your trip planner, the Internet, or travel bureau at your destination for available services. Your escort can also point you towards clubs and locales where singles are most likely to congregate.

✦

Check out learning vacations. This is becoming extremely popular with many Americans. Disney World and Fodor's Great American Learning Vacations both offer many discovery excursions for families and single adults. Give this a try, you'll be happy with the results!

✦

Go to a dude ranch. Cowboy country means lots of cowhands and men on horseback. Although families are the main visitors at the ranch, that's okay, it just means more cuties for you! There also are several outfits that offer classes for the wannabe cowboy where participants can actually take part in a cattle roundup. If you like your men in chaps, I suggest you sign up right now!

✦

Attend a baseball game at Camden Yards . . . or other well-known field and get to know male sports fans in other parts of the country.

✦

Teach something on a cruise ship. If you have a special talent, cruise lines are always looking for individuals to provide a variety of specialty classes. Not only do you get to travel to interesting destinations, but you will make many new friendships.

✦ ✦ ✦

12

GOING OUT ALONE

Women are always asking me, "Where can I go at night when I'm by myself?"

This, sadly, is an unfortunate reality of being single. Let's face it, going places alone when everyone else is in couples, is not easy. You feel self-conscious sitting by yourself with no one to talk to, wondering if everyone is looking at you. I hated going to places by myself for this very reason and, rather than venture out on my own, would end up spending night after night at home alone. But once I forced myself to do things by myself, I discovered most people don't even notice and if they do, it doesn't matter to them whether you are alone or not.

Going out by yourself does not have to be some dreaded, lonely experience. There are many places you can go where other people will also be by themselves.

The following sections will give you suggestions on dining alone and evening activities where you will be comfortable, even if you are unescorted. But first, here are a few tips that may help you before you head out on your own.

TIPS . . .

- **If you feel intimidated walking into some place . . .** go directly to the restroom, which gives you a chance to see who is there and where to sit if you decide to stay. Also, most bathrooms are in the back, giving you the opportunity to re-enter the room less conspicuously.

- **Arrive early, before it gets crowded . . .** and then stay for dinner. It's easier to walk into a room with a handful of people, plus you'll be part of the action as more fellows arrive.

- **If uncomfortable sitting by yourself, pretend you are waiting for someone . . .** we've all had to at one time or another and no one gives it a second thought. Or wear a suit and pretend you're on company time – business travelers are frequently out by themselves.

- **Go out on weekdays.** Usually less crowded and with fewer couples than weekends. You'll also find more men out with their buddies.

- **Ask to join someone.** If it's crowded and you see an empty seat at a large table with one or two people, ask if you might join them. Very few people will turn you down. Besides, most individuals have been alone at one time or another and can appreciate having someone to talk to when they are by themselves.

- **Avoid so-called singles bars and Friday happy hours.** If you want to have a drink find other alternatives, such as in a nice restaurant or hotel lounge.

- **Take a magazine to read or work on a crossword puzzle.** Men are less likely to approach you, if you are engrossed in a book.

- **Ask the host or hostess to seat other solo patrons with you.** You may not be the only one who would like someone to talk with.

- **Notice places where people are alone.** Men and women by themselves are more common than you think.

DINING ALONE

Try casual or family-style dining places . . . including neighborhood cafés, specialty and take out dining locations. Single men eat out a lot and prefer inexpensive, informal eateries. Just about any diner that says "Mom's" or "Good Eats" is a good possibility.

✦

Go where there's a salad bar. These are very conducive for talking with other customers while filling up your plate with good things to eat.

✦

Reserve a table in a hotel dining room. Hotel guests dining alone are a common sight. Pretend you're on a business trip and have dinner in the nicest restaurant . . . on the boss, of course! If you have an occasion to engage a man who is by himself in a conversation, by all means, do so. Many businessmen who spend a lot of time on the road will welcome a friendly visit.

✦

Dine outside at a waterfront restaurant. Go early before the crowds arrive, you can always occupy yourself by watching the boating activities. Dinner houses near marinas will be busy at day's end, especially if there's an open-air dining area.

✦

Spend time at places that are conducive for talking with other patrons. Many people frequent coffeehouses, bakeries and neighborhood cafés for this very reason. So, you be there, too!

✦

Visit the airport and dine in one of the restaurants. It's really easy to strike up a conversation . . . "Where are you headed?" is a good start. This is a great place when you're by yourself!

✦

Sit at a community table in a neighborhood café. Many small restaurants set aside a table for lone diners to sit together and is a super way to meet new people. If not offered, ask the manager to give it a try.

✦

Have dinner at the shopping mall. Many of us don't think twice about having lunch while shopping, so why not dinner. Make yourself visible and sit at an outside table. Malls with hotels nearby are also good prospects, as business travelers are more likely to be wandering around in the evening.

✦

Go to a diner or coffee shop . . . and sit at the counter with other customers who are by themselves. You can also wait for a fellow to enter a restaurant and take a seat, before going in and sitting next to him. If it worked for Mitzi, it will work for you!

✦

Buy a hot dog and watch a Little League game. Single fathers will be there watching their kids. Sit in the stands and cheer for one of the teams. Not only a sociable environment, but watching a group of youngsters field baseballs can be a kick. This has been one of my favorite means of meeting many nice fellows.

✦

Dine in the bar area of a restaurant. Most offer appetizers or limited menu items and usually have a TV tuned to news or sports. Not only is it cheaper for the guys to eat in the bar, but they can watch the game, too. You may also want to hang around for live entertainment later in the evening, if available.

✦

Eat at a health food store. Many have small cafés on the premises, so you can shop for healthy foods and then feast on a vegetarian meal. The individuals you meet are not only health conscious, but often fascinating individuals. Go ahead and talk to someone, you'll have an interesting conversation.

✦

Pretend you're traveling and have dinner at a truck stop. These stopovers are filled with truckers who are by themselves and would welcome some friendly chitchat. You'll also see solitary diners at 24-hour restaurants near freeway offramps and motels.

✦

Attend a banquet or dinner meeting. As mentioned earlier, many business and specialty groups meet regularly for dinner and welcome newcomers. Once you know when these meetings are being held, there will be plenty of evenings where you won't have to wonder what to do!

✦

Find a café where you order from a walk-up counter. These less formal eateries are often frequented by people dining alone. Make this a favorite haunt and see who you meet!

✦

Order a nice meal at a casino. If you're near a gambling establishment, this is another spot where you don't have to be concerned about being with someone.

✦

On a nice day sit at an outside café. Alfresco spots next to busy pedestrian areas are great, giving you the opportunity to also chat with passers-by.

✦

Ask to be seated with a group at a Japanese restaurant. Join other diners at a circular table (made popular by a well-known restaurant chain) and watch the chef's performance as he prepares their meals with a lot of fanfare. And, you don't need a date to enjoy this!

✦

Get in line at a cafeteria-style restaurant. Another popular place for solo males. If it's crowded and you see someone alone at a table, ask if you may join him. There's no harm in asking and the meal may turn out better than you expected!

✦

Go online at an Internet café. These informal eateries are springing up all over the country. Get a bite to eat while you ride the Information Superhighway . . . and check out some of the websites I've already mentioned.

✦

Have dinner at an athletic club. One of many amenities offered to members. Most clubs have casual dining and some, more elegant faire. Many men, after completing their evening workout, like to get something to eat before heading home. So make sure you're there, too!

✦

Fill up your plate with complimentary appetizers. Many places, especially Mexican restaurants, offer free food in the bar for a specified time after the workday. Single men will stop by on their way home, as it's one less meal they have to worry about. You will be more comfortable if you get there early, so you are not walking into a room full of fellows.

✦

Picnic in front of your house or apartment . . . and chat with passers-by. If you come in contact with someone of interest, invite them to join you for a snack and a little conversation. You just never know what may result from this one neighborly gesture!

✦

Dine in the clubhouse at a golf course. In addition to informal food service, many have more formal dining facilities. Either choice offers a good opportunity to meet men, especially during the summer months when daylight savings allows golfers to play later at night.

✦

Order a quick meal at a concession stand . . . at a park, flea market, fair or other community event. Then be part of whatever activities are going on.

✦

Stop by a roadside inn. Take an evening drive to a nearby town and have dinner along the way. Casual restaurants in rural areas have a lot of potential, as there often will be several friendly, unattached gents inside.

✦

Order a California roll at a sushi bar. Most Japanese restaurants offer this in their lounges and many single people stop by on their way home from work to enjoy this ethnic delicacy. You can, too!

✦

Enjoy a moveable feast. This is best done in busy commercial areas where there are many eateries to chose from. Stop at several spots, starting for example, with a salad from a deli, a chicken entree from another place and finally, splurging with dessert from a bakery or ice cream parlor. The more places you go, the better your chances of bumping into someone along the way . . . and, if you do, ask him to join you at your next stop.

✦

Fill a picnic basket and spend an evening outdoors. Find a spot near a waterfront park or other busy area of town. If you are so inclined, bring some music, light a candle and pour a glass of wine. Now you're ready to converse with others out on this warm night.

✦

Grab a bite to eat at a local college . . . the student center is the hub for many older adults during the evening. So, find a table where a gentleman is sitting and say, "Hi!"

✦

Sample some food at a hospital cafeteria. For most of us this is the last place we think of going, but they are filled with doctors and interns . . . and many are single.

✦

Patronize eateries within a short walk of a hospital. Frequented by hospital personnel and visitors looking for a change of pace from cafeteria food. And, I'm sure someone would enjoy a friendly conversation!

✦

Get something to eat at a bowling alley . . . and stick around to watch the activity. Be ready to laugh a lot, as a group of male bowlers can be a lot of fun!

✦

Take yourself to a gourmet restaurant. Dress elegantly, hold your head up high and have a great time. If you get a few stares, so what! Pretend to be a wealthy eccentric . . . or just be yourself, a self-confident woman enjoying an elegant meal.

✦ ✦ ✦

AFTER HOURS

The following ideas are for those who just want to get out, have some fun, be around people and perhaps meet a man or two.

Spend an evening at a nice hotel . . . particularly those with conference facilities. The more men staying at or visiting the hotel, the better it is. It's quite probable that once the function is over, some of the attendees will stop for a nightcap in the lounge. In any event, the more things you do and time you spend there, the greater the odds of meeting several male guests. **$** And, of course, the more expensive the hotel, the more likely you are to meet gentlemen of means.

✦

Try dancing in a hotel nightclub or disco. Many hotel visitors will be by themselves, so you needn't feel uncomfortable going it alone. Why not give it a try and see what happens!

✦

Pull on a pair of boots and line dance at a country/western spot. You don't need a partner, just get in line and follow along!

✦

Go to a pub or restaurant and sit at the bar . . . and chat with the bartender or the guy sitting next to you. Really . . . you can do it!

✦

Attend a professional sporting event. Those fortunate to be near pro teams can enjoy this activity. I don't have to remind you that sports are well-attended by men of all ages. Baseball is a good choice as there are lots of male spectators and the season lasts several months. Plus, it's something you can do ala carte and no one will even notice.

✦

Go somewhere and listen to music. Many restaurant and hotel lounges have live entertainment, so relax with a cocktail and enjoy the music. Rock 'n' roll, blues groups and jazz combos will attract the most men.

✦

Find a busy coffee bar . . . a good alternative to establishments serving alcohol. Sit at the counter and don't be shy about talking with other patrons. Besides, you might actually enjoy yourself!

✦

Enjoy a high school football game. This is your best bet to be around single fathers and many alumni who support their old alma mater. Seating is usually on a first come, first served basis, so look for an empty seat next to someone interesting.

✦

Watch televised sports in a sports bar or restaurant lounge. Many have big-screen TVs for interested fans. During football season, watching *Monday Night Football* in a bar is a ritual for many single men. So, go early before the crowds arrive to secure a table or a spot at the bar. Plus, if there's an empty seat next to you, someone may join you.

✦

Spend time at a fitness club. I've already mentioned that these facilities are excellent sources for meeting men during the lunch hour. And even more fellows will be using the facilities after the workday. Depending on the type of club you join, there will be a variety of amenities and frequent social functions where members can meet each other. In addition to exercising, you can watch a handball or squash match, challenge someone to a game of racquetball, or grab a bite to eat in the snack bar or restaurant and get to know other club members.

✦

Attend a seminar or lecture. If you want to be around men, stick to subject matter that is of interest to them. In larger cities you can attend something almost every night of the week . . . and it's quite possible you could meet your future mate at one of them!

✦

Enjoy an activity at a local college. Get an event schedule and take in a seminar, sporting or musical presentation. Unescorted students frequently attend these functions and most are open to the public. So, go check it out . . . you might be surprised at who is there!

✦

Sit at a piano bar. You'll find lots of entertainers have a following, many of whom are unattached. Request a favorite song and sing along.

✦

Try your luck at a casino. For those with access to gaming houses, this is a great way to get out and interact with lots of people. If you would rather not gamble, you can listen to lounge entertainment or wander about until you see someone who catches your eye and then hang around and watch what he's playing.

✦

Attend a summer concert in the park. Look for a spot near a nice looking fellow or a group of adults. If you bring along food, invite those next to you to share it with you. Just be friendly . . . it really does work!

✦

Hang out at the airport. There are so many men and so many ways to meet them . . . you just can't beat it! Here are a few things you can do while you are there:
- *Find an empty seat* – and strike up a conversation with the fellow sitting next to you.
- *Stop in one of the many restaurants* – and talk with someone who is by himself.
- *Spend a few hours at one of the private airline clubs* (that is, if you've taken my advise and become a member).
- *Have a drink in one of the lounges* – and chat with travelers waiting for their flights.

✦

$ Find an auction to attend. Estate sales are usually held in the evening and is a fun way to pass the time. While previewing items visit with other potential bidders. Give it a try . . . I don't think you will be disappointed!

✦

Listen to live music at the bookstore. Many places offer entertainment to encourage customers to stay awhile. You can sit in a comfortable chair while you listen to the music or have a café au lait and something to nibble on in an adjacent coffee bar. Don't be surprised if you enjoy this so much, you will want to do it more than once.

✦

Get out on a nice summer night. Find a place to sit next to a busy walkway or stroll along and be friendly with other people out on this nice night. Don't think about it . . . just go do it!

✦

Enter a tournament or contest. Many pubs have competitions on certain nights of the week, such as backgammon, 8-ball, or darts. Call around to see what is available. If you don't want to participate, then watch those who are playing. Give it a try, this could be the difference between meeting someone or not.

✦ ✦ ✦

13

Getting People Together

I think people go to singles bars, because they don't know where else to go to meet someone. Based on what male friends have told me, they, too, wonder where to go to meet the opposite sex and are looking for ways to connect with someone special . . . just like you!

The following suggestions are geared to getting people together. I am convinced the more often you can get individuals into a fun setting, you'll start to see sparks. Give a few a try and see if you don't agree!

Auction off eligible men for a day or evening. This works really well for professional women who do not have time to meet a lot of men. Gather up a dozen or more guys willing to spend the day with the female who bids the most for him. Again, there are several benefits for you if you are the organizer: not only do you get to talk with *all* of the men as you convince them to be a part of this event, but you also will be helping other single women meet someone new. Hold the bidding gala at a restaurant or hotel with banquet facilities and donate all proceeds to charity. This may turn out to be so successful, that you will want to do this on a grander scale. You will be a huge hit for putting this on!

✦

Offer a dancing class for men . . . like country western, ballroom, or one of the current styles. Then gather up several of your girlfriends to be their partners. Be sure to switch around regularly, so everyone has a chance to meet everyone else. And, of course, if your advertising mentions that partners will be provided . . . you're sure to have a good turnout!

✦

Invite a few girlfriends and an equal number of men . . . to get together for dinner at a restaurant or at one of your homes (but only if the men are known to one or more women in your group – you want to be cautious with strangers). Place an ad that says something like, "Looking for single male entrepreneurs from 30-40 to meet with a group of female professionals." Also, post notices at sports clubs, office buildings, apartments and restaurants in the area. Ask male respondents a few questions that you've put together, so unsuitable fellows can be screened out. Once you pick out the gentlemen you'd like to meet, invite an equal number of ladies, too. The object is to remove the pressure of one-on-one meetings and if there are several people, it makes everyone feel more comfortable. Groups of four or six are best, but if you decide to invite more than that, have the men from each table switch seats at the end of the salad course, so that everyone has a chance to meet each other.

✦

Grab a few friends and attend a sporting event. This is when you'll want to get the girls together. Several unattached females at a ballgame will catch the eye of single guys from near and far. I guarantee, you'll have a blast!

✦

Encourage your friends to set you up with eligible men. "Oh, no, not the blind dates!" you scream. I know, they've been disastrous for most of us. But, don't give up, one of them could turn out to be "the one!" If you've had bad luck with blind dates, be more specific with your friends about what you are looking for, such as someone who loves classical music, likes to dance, or has an interest in gardening. Then you at least will have something in common to talk about.

✦

Pass on to your friends the guys you are not interested in. Even if you don't hit it off, someone else may find him interesting. I have several happily married friends who still thank me for introducing them to their husbands-to-be.

✦ ✦ ✦

LET'S HAVE A PARTY

I love parties and when I was single, my greatest challenge was making sure there would be several new male faces at each of my soirees. Nevertheless, a couple of girlfriends continued to complain about not meeting any new men at the parties.

"Okay, I'll come up with a new bunch of guys," I said assuredly, "just show up this weekend and you'll see!"

Now I've done it, I thought, I've promised my friends some new faces, but where was I going to find a dozen or so eligible men and on such short notice? As I sat pondering my dilemma, it suddenly it hit me, I know where to find them! And with that I made out the invitations.

When the big day came, many of the girls were surprised when they saw the same familiar faces.

"I knew it," one gal snidely commented, "it's going to be the same old group." As I was explaining that she should be patient, someone looked out the window and yelled, "Hey, everyone, it looks like there must be a fire. There's a huge hook-and-ladder out in front!" As they all scrambled toward the window, there was a knock at the front door.

"You must be from the Fire Department," I exclaimed, as I opened the door, "come on in, the party's about to begin!"

Well, as you may have guessed, the party was a huge success. Not only did more than a dozen unattached firemen join us that evening, but we had more new faces at future parties, including several buddies of our new-found friends.

Oh, and by the way, the boys from the firehouse were thrilled that we had invited them, but best of all, they loved meeting so many nice women. And the end result: many dates, a couple of new friendships and one marriage. ·

It doesn't take much to be creative, to think about where groups of men congregate and then how you can meet them. If there's several unattached fellows at your fitness club, invite them to a mixer. Or better yet, put up a notice inviting *all* the eligible guys who work out at the gym. Remember, you can never have too many men! The following party ideas have worked for me and my friends, perhaps they will work for you.

Invite lots of fellows. Make the party fun or give it a theme. Try something different or unique, so that these new people will be intrigued enough to show up. Send invitations to the local fire station, as I did, or other male groups, like a softball team, chess club, or business group. Hand an invitation to someone you see frequently at the deli or in the elevator at work and ask him to bring a buddy or two. Put up notices where you live, at your office, the athletic or golf club you belong to. And have several of your friends give out party information, too. It doesn't take a rocket scientist to figure out, the more new people who come, the more individuals there are for you to meet!

✦

Host a " bring someone new" party. The concept is for men to bring another male and women to bring another female. Invite a few more guys than gals, but not so many that the number of males will be lopsided, otherwise the fellows that do come will not appreciate it. Start the festivities with a few get-acquainted games. For example, have everyone write their name and a few descriptive words about themselves on a piece of paper, like "Mike Smith, great dancer," "Carol Jones, architect," "Stan Evans, chess player." Place all male names in a container and female in another, each party-goer draws a name of the opposite sex and then tries to find that person. Give this a try, it will be a *very* successful mixer.

✦

Organize a reunion. Contact friends from your high school or college alma mater, a group from the old neighborhood, or ex-co-workers. Many things can happen over the years, people get divorced, spouses die and with any kind of luck, you might have an opportunity to rekindle an old romance. It's worth a try and besides, it'll be nice to reacquaint yourself with an old friend.

✦

Have a potluck. This is a dinner party where everyone brings something to eat or drink. I recently read about a group of twenty adults that have been getting together for the past ten years. They meet every week and the main constant . . . everyone knows there will always be a place to go on Monday nights. People have come and gone over the years and two of them ended up marrying each other. By the way, single men will love this, because the most common complaint I hear, is their having to eat out so many nights a week.

✦

Enjoy a gourmet dining and fine wine gathering . . . and have epicurean meals at member's homes or dine at different restaurants with selected wines at each course. You may want to contact wineries or wine merchants, as they will often present special tastings for the group.

✦

Give a slumber party. Everyone arrives in "jammies" and brings a sleeping bag and depending on the weather, sleep inside or outside. Play games, sing songs, tell stories and, of course, make sure you have a few pranks to pull.

✦

Invite friends to a "Kids Only" affair. Party-goers bring their favorite children's toy or game (or you can provide marbles, Jacks, Pick-up-Sticks, Tiddlywinks, Old Maid, Cootie, etc.). Have competitions in each toy category and give out prizes apropos to the theme. Food should include hot dogs and lots of desserts, including chocolate pudding and cookies. Guaranteed to be a great time . . . this has been a huge favorite with both male and female friends of mine.

✦

Stage a talent show. Everyone participates, but real talent isn't necessary. In fact, the less one has, the better it is . . . silliness and fun should be everyone's goal. You may want to add a few "talent" suggestions to the invitations to get your guest's creative juices flowing, like "Bring your best singing voice, try tap dancing or juggling, put on a magic act, get a partner and tumble, or recite a poem . . . any talent, good or bad, will do." Needless to say this has been another big favorite.

✦

Have a beach party. If you don't have a shoreline nearby, dig a hole or make your own barbeque with rocks and bricks. Play typical games like horseshoes, badminton, or volleyball. If you live in an apartment, a local park or nearby schoolyard will also suffice for playing games.

✦

Host a "Tom Jones" BBQ . . . remember the eating scene in the movie *"Tom Jones?"* The invitations should state that everyone wear grubby clothes or foul weather gear. The idea is to barbeque some meat or chicken and place the BBQ sauce in a bowl in the center of the dining table. Then dip into the sauce and eat . . . absolutely no silverware allowed! It will be messy, but everyone will have a lot of fun.

✦

Organize a campout in your backyard. Pitch a tent and invite a few friends to come over. Build a campfire and roast weinies, then follow with toasted marshmallows. And, of course, you must sit around the fire singing songs and telling ghost stories.

✦

Invite a few fellows over for a game of 5-card Stud or Draw Poker. If you do not know that a full house beats a flush, get someone to teach you or get a computer game and learn the basics. Seek out several prospects from your office, neighborhood, or a club you belong to. For a friendly game, keep the stakes low (nickel, dime, quarter) and have plenty of snacks and beverages available. I guarantee you will have a great time . . . in fact, some of my fondest memories are with the boys on poker nights!

✦

Have a gambling party. Most major cities have companies that will bring all the equipment and operate it for you. As this will take up a lot of room, you may want to use the clubhouse at an apartment complex or rent some space. And donate any money the "house" makes to charity.

✦

Cook a Thanksgiving dinner with all the trimmings in July. As you know by now, anytime a single guy can get a good meal, he'll be there. Make it just as much fun and festive as the real thing . . . and you're sure to please.

✦

Have an old cinema night and watch several old comedies. A few male favorites are The Marx Brothers, The Three Stooges, or a good cult movie, like *The Adventures of Buckaroo Bonzai*. Another fun idea is to rent a 3D flick, and be sure there are enough glasses to go around.

✦

Play Hide and Seek . . . or "Spot Tag" outside in the dark. Lots of trees will make it even more fun or if there is not enough room where you live, go to the park. People will enjoy this so much that they will be talking about it for months. Suggest everyone bring a flashlight, so they can see where they are going. You can make up the rules as you go, but basically, the person who is "it" covers his/her eyes while everyone hides. Then as "it" spots someone, that person has to race back to tag "home" before "it" gets there, otherwise they become the person who is "it."

✦

Go on a scavenger hunt. List 20-30 items that can be found around the house, including a few hard-to-find objects. Set a time limit and send teams into the neighborhood. The group returning with the most items wins. Everyone should be in pairs, so find out ahead of time which fellow each of your girlfriends would like to be coupled with.

✦ ✦ ✦

ORGANIZE FUN ACTIVITIES

Stage a mini-Olympics. Choose five to ten events for individual competition. A few events to consider using: racquetball, tennis, golf (9 holes), baseball throw, homerun hitting derby, bowling, short and long running races, one-on-one basketball, football accuracy throw and swimming events. Depending on the number of venues, plan on it taking a day or weekend to complete. You will need several girlfriends to help you, as each event will need overseeing, not to mention how thirsty and hungry these fellows will get. At the completion of the "Olympics," have a banquet to present trophies and prizes.

✦

Find several pals who like to ski and hit the slopes. During the winter months, this is where you'll find men in large numbers. So get moving and put yourself where the boys will be!

✦

Organize a bicycle trip . . . to a destination half-a-day's ride away or an overnighter somewhere. This is a great activity for bringing people together and interacting in a comfortable environment. Just be sure that wherever you go, they know how many people to expect. A couple dozen folks could cause havoc for some places.

✦

Get together a group of girlfriends to go camping. Campgrounds near popular outdoor recreational areas are your best bet. Find a spot near a group of guys and you'll have way too much fun!

✦

Coordinate a road rally. The idea is for everyone to end up at an unknown location. Give everyone a map and a list of cryptic clues, like "from the MacDonald's on Front St., drive 5.2 miles and turn left, continue until you see children at play, if you pass two white houses in a row you've gone too far . . ." Be sure to give a cell phone number in case someone should get lost. And once everyone reaches the destination, have a dinner party, picnic, or some other social event.

✦

Gather up some friends for a baseball game. This is a good opportunity to invite firemen or males from a sports group to join you and a few friends. Those who don't want to play can act as cheerleaders. And, of course, have a barbeque or party afterwards, then you can visit with that cutie you've been eyeing!

✦

Put on a kite flying contest at the park ... offer prizes for smallest, largest, most unusual, highest, or longest flying. You will have lots of men participating, especially if you contact local men's clubs, sporting groups, restaurants, taverns and possibly a couple of corporations. The more of these groups involved, the more men will be there.

✦

Organize tricycle races. Everyone brings their own trike, which can be customized. As long as it has three wheels, anything goes. In addition to winners of sprints and endurance races, award prizes for slowest, biggest, smallest and most creative. This is a really fun event that will attract lots of fun-loving fellows!

✦

Have frog jumping contests and turtle races. The zanier the function, the more fun it will be. Present awards for best dressed, longest jump, fastest, or the "beetlebaum" trophy for the slowest critter. Each participant brings a frog or turtle and races begin by putting competitors in the middle of a circle. To get the turtles moving, suggest taping sticks to their backs and dangling lettuce or other enticements in front of the little guy's head. And after the festivities, please release the frogs back into their natural habitats.

✦ ✦ ✦

14

AND IF THAT'S
NOT ENOUGH

Well, we're nearing the end, but I still have several dozen more suggestions that didn't fit into any of the categories in previous chapters. And just because they didn't work somewhere else, doesn't mean they're not good, too!

Put together information about bachelor entrepreneurs in your area . . . and submit it either as a newspaper or magazine article. Or you might put together a booklet that single women in your community can purchase. In either case, contact several unmarried gentleman, letting each one know what you are doing and that you would like to include a photo and short article about him. Suggest interviewing him over dinner, so you can talk with him face-to-face. This will give you an opportunity to find out his interests and what he does in his spare time. If nothing else, you'll know where and what each of them likes to do in their free time and you can do the same. Then when you bump into one of them, you'll have something to talk to him about. It will take a bit of work to find out who the bachelors are. Check with your local newspaper, it may already have a database on single entrepreneurs, otherwise you'll have to contact several companies and find out the marital status of their CEO and other executive officers. But believe me, the work will be well worth the effort, especially if you wind up meeting your future mate.

◆

Get a tatoo. Lots of men do this, just look at some of the professional athletes that have decorated their bodies . . . there's hours of work on those arms and legs. And while you're there, you're bound to meet someone who is a bit daring, too!

◆

Subscribe to an alumni newsletter . . . either your high school or college association. Find out about upcoming events and how to get in touch with classmates you've lost contact with. This is a super opportunity to connect with a few old friends and who knows, one of them may look even better now!

◆ ◆ ◆

EVENINGS AND WEEKENDS

Before I discovered how easy it was to get out and meet people, I would often spend an entire weekend at home and not talk to a solitary soul. Come Monday morning I could hardly wait to get to the office and visit with the first person I saw.

If you, too, spend a lot of time alone, especially on the weekends, try some of the following ideas and before you know it, you won't be lonely anymore.

CLOSE TO HOME . . .

It's the weekend, so go out for breakfast! As mentioned earlier, a local breakfast place with good food will be packed with men during the morning hours, especially on the weekend . . . so, what are you waiting for?

✦

Sip on a cappuccino at a bakery or coffeehouse. Spend a few hours next Saturday morning relaxing while you read the paper. Not only will you discover that this weekend ritual is a must for many individuals, but if you do this on a regular basis, you will begin to meet plenty of people . . . why not go and see for yourself!

✦

Enjoy alfresco dining in busy pedestrian areas. These outdoor cafés are great for visiting with other customers and passers-by. And you just never know where a friendly conversation will lead.

✦

Place yourself in public areas. Situate yourself along busy walkways, in parks and other activity areas. Smile at people as they pass by and ask how their day's going. The more you do it, the more people you meet . . . and if anyone can do this, why not you!

✦

Solve crossword puzzles while waiting in public. Try this instead of reading a book or magazine, then ask the guy nearest you, "What's a five-letter word for . . ."

✦

Rummage through a garage sale. Especially at apartment complexes and other neighborhoods where singles live. Also, look for sales in the classifieds that mention items, like athletic equipment or tools. This will draw a large number of male treasure seekers.

✦

Have minor auto repairs and servicing done on Saturday mornings . . . like getting your tires rotated, an oil change, or a new battery. Most of us put off doing car stuff, but don't – the waiting room will be absolutely loaded with guys. This is such a great way to meet men you may want to ask your friends and neighbors if you can take in their cars, too!

✦

Enjoy an outdoor concert. You will frequently find open-air performances during the summer months in most communities. And although there will be a lot of families, you will also find quite a few fellows, either by themselves or with a couple of buddies. So, pick out a spot near one of them . . . and see what happens!

✦

Visit a museum. Look for those specializing in male themes, like vintage cars, antique airplanes, sports memorabilia, or maritime exhibits. If you see a man by himself, he is probably unattached . . . and you know what to do next!

✦

Plop down a beach chair and sit by the water. Look for spots where a lot of activity is going on, particularly near a group of adults. If there are several fellows playing catch or volleyball, be sure you're close enough to get in on the action if the ball goes astray.

✦

$ Put change in expired parking meters . . . particularly if it's an expensive automobile or one that men often drive. Write a note on the back of your business card, telling them what you've done and place it on their windshield. If the car's owner is single, he just might call and ask to thank you over a cup of coffee. Although not everyone will contact you . . . all it takes is one!

✦

Spend an afternoon in the downtown district . . . where many local residents will be milling about. You can do a little shopping, get something to eat, or find a place to sit and people watch, anyone of which will provide hours of entertainment. And, of course, look for men who are by themselves . . . remember to smile, you just may catch his eye as he walks by!

✦ ✦ ✦

MORE PLACES MEN FREQUENT

Go to happy hour. Many restaurants offer free food in the bar during the late afternoon when business is slow. Single guys will be there eating as much as possible, as it's one less meal they have to worry about. Locations near commercial districts will have a lot of businessmen, usually between 5 and 6 p.m. You'll also find that Monday through Thursday evenings are the best nights to go for freebies. Go early and get a spot at the bar, before the crowds arrive.

✦

Sample beer at a microbrewery. These small distilleries are very popular in some parts of the country. Since men are the main consumers of beer, this obviously is a great place to find them. And the food's not bad either!

✦

Frequent neighborhood taverns. As depicted on *Cheers* these local pubs are often the social hub for many bachelors who live in the vicinity. But the best part is once you meet one of them, you'll meet everyone else!

✦

Look for restaurants or pubs with live entertainment. Rock 'n' roll and blues groups will be the most popular with the male set. If you want to hear good music and be around a lot of men, you can't beat this!

✦

Go to a sports bar . . . especially for *Monday Night Football* and when locally broadcast games are on television. These spots will always be popular with the fellows, so do yourself a favor and make it one of your frequent haunts, as well.

✦

Order a burger in a tavern during lunch. These places may make the best hamburgers and fries in town and are extremely popular with the opposite sex, and it is not uncommon to see several fellows by themselves. Also, another good thing to consider is that during the day, the "pick-up" element is almost non-existent.

✦

Patronize eateries and pubs near sporting venues. These will be very busy before and after games when spectators will be there in large numbers. And you already know that men outnumber women at most sporting events, so the odds will be with you.

✦

Visit after hours spots where professional players go following the game. Single guys from the home club and the visiting team usually have a favorite place where they like to unwind before retiring for the night. Get a friend to go with you and be there when they arrive.

✦

Discover where firemen and policemen hang out. Oftentimes there will be one or two places that they tend to frequent. Once you become familiar with their favorite haunts, you'll have an opportunity to meet lots of these uniformed cuties!

✦

Go to pubs or sports bars that are patronized by weekend athletes. Once the guys have finished playing, they often go somewhere to celebrate. If you see a group playing Rugby or baseball, find out where they're going afterwards . . . and be there, too.

✦

Locate biker bars and diners. Active motorcycle groups often get together for dinner and comradery on a weekly basis and will usually patronize a couple of favorite places. Contrary to what you may be thinking, these are not the black leather jacket, rowdy stereotypes that are associated with biker gangs. Instead you will find men and women just like yourself. But you won't know this until you go and meet a few of them!

✦ ✦ ✦

THINGS TO DO WITH KIDS

There are many places you can go with your children and also meet men. If you do not have young ones, that's okay, just get a few neighborhood kids together or borrow a niece or nephew and try some of the following suggestions.

Take a tour of the fire or police department. Call ahead to set up a time to take the group through the station. While the children are touring the facilities, you will have a chance to talk with the boys. Good-sized cities will have several locations, so you can make a visit to each one and meet even more fellows!

✦

Coach or referee a youth sport . . . such as Little League, Pop Warner, or a soccer team. Not only will you get to know single fathers, but it will put you at the recreation park where you will come in contact with other guys who are using the facilities. Look for refereeing and coaching clinics put on by the recreation department. If you find one to attend, you'll also discover another benefit . . . participants in these classes almost always are men!

✦

Go to a pizza parlor or other family-style dining spot . . . particularly those that are frequented by fellows who play in men's leagues in the evening. After the game is completed, many team members will hit the pizzeria for "pies and suds." And then you'll be there when they arrive!

✦

Find a wrestling match. Young boys love this staged sport and while watching the antics in the ring, you can chat with the guys sitting around you.

✦

Zoom around a go-cart track. This is another activity that boys of all ages enjoy. Many tracks are also part of a larger complex that offer arcade games, batting cages and sometimes miniature golf. Although this is a family affair, you will find plenty of dads and their sons participating in all the activities.

✦

Attend a sporting event . . . any will do. The more games you go to, the more your kids will love it, and the more chances you'll have to meet male sports fans. Sounds like a win-win situation to me!

✦

Look for an RC model show. In addition to lots of little boys, there will be lots of big boys, too!

✦

Grab a pole and take a kid fishing. Find out from the local tackle shop where the best fishing is and plan an outing there. And don't worry, if you don't know how to bait a hook, there will be plenty of fishermen nearby who will gladly show you how!

✦

Score the highest points at a video arcade. Expect the guys to be younger, mainly in their twenties, but the ones who are there will be unattached. The games may take a lot of quarters, but it doesn't cost a cent to hang around and watch someone play.

✦

Take your child to a golf driving range. This is a great opportunity to be around male golfers, even if you don't want to try it yourself. And don't be shy about asking a handsome male to give your son or daughter a few tips. If you do this once or twice a week, it won't be long before you'll get to know a lot of these fellows!

✦

Spend time at the park. Play catch with your child and when the ball goes over your head, be sure to smile at the gentleman who throws it back to you. Who knows, maybe he'd like to play catch, too!

✦

Go to a trading card show. Yet another activity that dads do with their children. Plus, you will find many eligible bachelors also collect trading cards and other sports memorabilia.

✦

Attend a soap box derby. A very popular activity where fathers participate with their sons and daughters and chances are very good there will be several single dads, too!

✦

Practice your swing at the batting cages. In addition to being very popular with many men and their kids, there will also be several fellows by themselves practicing their batting technique.

If you need help with your timing, maybe one of them will offer a few tips and before you know it, you will have a big hit!

✦

If you have children, try Parents Without Partners. Even though women usually outnumber the men at PWP functions, there are many single fathers who do attend. Social activities include events both with and without children.

✦

$ Set up outside a bank in an affluent area . . . for your son's or daughter's cookie drive. What a great way to help out the kids and meet well-to-do men at the same time!

✦ ✦ ✦

DOG DAYS

Enter your purebred in a dog show. You'll find many local exhibitions to attend. Pay attention to the working class and sporting breeds, they will have the most men attached to them. And by all means, plan on attending the national Westminster Kennel Club's show held annually during May in New York. This is the largest of its kind and if you love dogs and the men who own them, you won't want to miss this!

✦

Grab a leash and walk your dog. If you don't have a dog, offer to walk your neighbor's . . . and don't forget the pooper scooper! By the way, a daily walk around your neighborhood will eventually lead to many new friendships. And don't be surprised if one day that fellow who lives a few blocks away asks if you and your pal might like to come over and visit with him. It could happen!

✦

Take your dog to obedience class. Oftentimes instructors will keep the larger canines separate from the smaller ones. Since guys generally prefer big dogs, you'll have a better chance of meeting someone if your pooch is also a large breed.

✦

Teach your puppy to catch a Frisbee . . . and then enter him in a contest. By the way, it takes a lot of time to teach Fido how to catch it, so look for fellows and their mutts practicing at parks and playing fields. Here's your chance to be around these incredible dogs and their best friends.

✦

Go to the "dogs only" area of the park . . . and watch a man playing with his pal. Those who have four-legged buddies will take them to an open area and romp with them. You will often see dozens of men playing with their pets. Use this opportunity to talk to someone about how good his dog is or ask him questions about the canine's breed, disposition, and so on. The more interest you show in his dog, the more interest he may show in you!

✦

Raise Rottweilers or other protective breeds. Men prefer the more macho dogs and will be the main purchasers. If you offer these breeds for sale, men will come to your location to look at your puppies. Not only will this give you an opportunity to talk with him, but you can get his number and follow-up with phone calls or stop by to check on the puppy he bought from you. And perhaps later, you can breed one of yours with his . . . and watch the relationship grow!

✦

Save a pet from the SPCA or Humane Society . . . and take him for daily walks and romps in the out-of-doors. Any excuse to get outside and be around others is a good thing. Not only will you have a great companion, but people will want to stop and talk to you about your new pooch.

✦

Have a birthday party for your pet . . . and invite some of the individuals you've met and their dogs. Give a little toy to every critter and be sure to have plenty of food and drink for their owners.

✦

Visit with people out walking their dogs. Even if you don't have a four-legged friend, you can still talk with dog owners. They love having discussions about their best friend, so don't hesitate to ask questions about the breed or tell him how cute it is. This may be just the catalyst for a budding relationship!

✦

Watch a canine field trial event. *Extremely* popular with sportsmen and is a very important event for those who use their dogs for hunting and want to show off the training it has received. Check with the American Kennel Club or the Internet for information on events in your vicinity.

✦ ✦ ✦

START A SMALL BUSINESS

This section is for the woman who is willing to take a chance with a new career or has the time or initiative for a part-time job to cater to the needs of bachelors. Try to think of a service you can offer that helps someone whose time is limited and particularly those where you will come in contact with single men. Here are a few ideas to get you started.

Advertise your service . . . or send information to some of the previously mentioned businesses that are predominately male, like engineering, legal and software firms. You can also put flyers on cars in office parking lots. If they are there after hours, they are probably the ones who need this the most.

✦

$ Personal services business for men. I call this "Rent-a-Wife" (or for the well-to-do, a "personal concierge service"). This is for the single man who needs errands and chores done while he is at the office or away from home. Services you could provide:
  • *Shopping/errand service* – grocery shopping, personal gifts, prescription or laundry pickup and delivery.
  • *Maid service* – house cleaning, washing and ironing of clothes.

- *Indoor plant maintenance* – potting up plants, replacing dead plants, watering and fertilizing.
- *House sitting* – taking care of plants or picking up the mail, etc.
- *Taking pets for a walk* – a much needed task that he will be very grateful for.
- *Make alterations or minor repairs to clothing* – like sewing on buttons.

✦

Airport commuter. Since men are the primary business travelers during the week, they use shuttles the most and this is a good way to interact with them. You will pick them up at their home or office and deliver them to the airport terminal, or vice versa. And once you know where he lives or works, you can frequent establishments in his locale and when you see him again you can start the conversation with, "Don't I know you?"

✦

Offer an inventory service. This is where you go into homes or businesses and make a permanent record of their valuables and assets on videotape. You can also engrave all theft-prone items with social security or tax ID numbers. Besides, what better way to find out where they live and see what some of their interests are by what you see around their home.

✦

Meal preparation. This service requires preparing meals and leaving it in the client's refrigerator or a crock pot. Make enough so there will be plenty of leftovers. You won't believe the number of guys who will love to have this done for them!

✦

$ Make travel arrangements for the outdoorsman. You don't have to get a travel agent's license to do this, as you are only doing the coordinating. Locate a few special adventures through a travel planner or outfitter and get the word out, like Elk hunting in Western Canada, spring training for their favorite baseball team, or bareboat sailing in the Caribbean.

✦

Open a consignment shop catering to men. Items to carry include clothing, sports equipment, tools and other articles of male interest. Clientele will primarily be men . . . and that's the point, isn't it!

✦

Party planning . . . for single men and businesses. You will coordinate all the food, decorations, catering, bartending and entertainment. Plus, this will put you at the function where you will meet some of their friends and associates.

✦

Offer services for small businesses . . . and cater to the small entrepreneur. This will enable you to meet the owners and their employees. You can offer such services as Internet or library research, data entry, word processing, manuscript typing, light bookkeeping, temporary clerical help, or errand running.

✦

Sell snacks and lunch items to construction sites or office buildings. This is another good opportunity to meet people in the workforce. Get permission first and offer beverages, sandwiches, cookies, fruit and other snacks. Not only profitable, but after several weeks, you will meet a lot of fellows.

✦

Turn your house into a bed and breakfast . . . for male travelers. Even though couples usually use B&Bs, if you live in the right place and cater to single men, emphasizing male activities, it just might work.

✦

$ Concierge service for an upscale apartment building. Post notices or send out flyers to prospective clients in the complex. See page 185 for personal services you can provide.

✦

Be a disc jockey for a party. For those of you with an ability to ad lib and a great R & B or Rock 'n' Roll collection, this is ideal for you. Find out the type of music desired and any favorite artists or songs they'd like to hear. Then practice your DJ voice and come up with fun, zany verbiage to use. Not only will you meet most of the party-goers, but you will have way too much fun!

✦

Learn to bartend and hire out your services . . . this a great way to meet men. Not only do they hang around the "drink" table, but you will be included in the party, and that means interaction with lots of different people. Send brochures to businesses, or contact caterers, florists and party planners.

✦

Start a catering business. Again, this is a wonderful way to come in contact with a variety of people. Advertise through party supply outlets, grocery stores, deli's and florists. Get a couple of your single friends to give you a hand with food preparation, decorating and as hostesses. You will all benefit from the results!

✦

$ Manicure a bachelor's landscape. Many wealthy gentlemen use yard maintenance to keep their grounds looking nice and if you enjoy gardening, it might as well be you who's doing the work. Plus, on Saturday mornings when you're working in his yard, you'll have an opportunity to get to know him better.

✦ ✦ ✦

SERVICES MEN USE

Have your hair done in a salon that caters to both men and women. Some salons keep the ladies and gentlemen separate, others do not, patronize the latter. Find out when male customers regularly come in and try to schedule your appointment around that time with the adjacent stylist. If you are on good terms with your hairdresser, he or she can help you with this.

✦

$ Have your nails done at the same time that a man is getting a manicure. Many affluent men enjoy being pampered and this is one of their favorite indulgences.

✦

Stop by the cleaners before or after work. If you see a fellow dropping off or picking up his shirts, chances are pretty good he's unattached. If he is leaving his laundry, make a mental note of when it will be done and try to be there after work on that day. You just might get lucky and bump into him again. The counter worker will know who the regular customers are and can give you more information on when they usually come in.

✦

Wash and dry your clothes at a laundromat . . . next to a bar or restaurant. That's where most guys will be while their wash is finishing. Maybe you should wait there, too!

✦ ✦ ✦

SERENDIPITY

Serendipity is defined by Webster's Dictionary as "an ability for discovering new and interesting things by accident." Try one of the following activities and you may end up doing just that!

Take a drive along a lake or river . . . and stop at a waterfront restaurant for a drink on the terrace. Outside areas overlooking the water, especially in the afternoons and early evenings, will usually lead to many "sightings." If you are unfamiliar with areas near water activities, this is your chance to see how popular these spots can be.

✦

Get some exercise and put on a pair of inline skates. Lots of men are into this sport . . . and you can be, too!

✦

Grab a sketch pad and draw. This is a good one for you artists. Pick out a group of men playing ball or a fellow romping with his dog as your subject matter. It won't be long before one of them comes over to see what you're doing. And then be sure to get his number or business card so you can contact him again once the drawing is completed. By the way, if drawing is not your forte, you can always call it abstract!

✦ ✦ ✦

TAKE A WALK . . .

Mosey around a nearby park and watch the activity. Once there, you will find many occasions to be friendly with lots of people. And don't be too quick to leave, as you never know when a group of guys are planning to stop by to play ball . . . and you don't want to miss that!

✦

Spend time along the waterfront. I love commercial areas near the water. Nice evenings will always find lots of people walking around as they take advantage of the remaining hours of sunlight. If you encounter someone interesting, stop and talk with him. All it takes is a big smile and a little conversation . . . which may be the difference between meeting someone special or not!

✦

Wander through a college campus. Colleges are like small communities with places to eat and relax while conversing with other students. You will find many older academics and working adults attending evening and weekend classes, so get a cup of coffee from the canteen and see who is sitting in the lounge.

✦

Find a popular walking trail and take an afternoon stroll. The key word here is "popular." Use this time to check out areas where men may be recreating or playing sports and head in that direction to see what you find!

✦

Take off your shoes and go barefoot on the beach. Early mornings will find hardy souls looking for shells and other interesting objects that have washed ashore. This also is a popular time to see runners and men with their dogs.

✦

Go on a walk along a busy boardwalk or near high-activity areas. Downtown commercial districts offer many good possibilities of meeting other individuals who are out and about. If nothing else, smile at everyone you pass and I'll bet you'll be conversing with someone before the day is done.

✦

Get up early and enjoy a beautiful sunrise. Until you've tried this, you won't know what a great way this is to meet early risers, not to mention seeing the beauty of this peaceful time of day. Once you know where morning folks can be found, it's your job to keep going there at the same time until people start acknowledging you. Really . . . it does work!

✦

Find a popular jogging path and walk around. The best time to go is right after work, the next best is weekend mornings. Even though you will not be running, you still have an opportunity to acknowledge others as you stroll along. It worked for me and it will work for you, too!

✦

Walk to the nearest ice cream parlor . . . and indulge in an enormous banana split. (That is, if you've walked far enough to justify the extra calories!) Ice cream parlors are very busy in the evenings after dinner. Besides, if a fellow doesn't love ice cream, he's probably not worth meeting!

✦

Stroll along a waterfront promenade . . . and visit with residents sitting outside enjoying the day. It is not uncommon for them to invite someone walking by to join them for a drink and a little chitchat, especially in the late afternoon, when the crowds are dissipating. You'll meet lots of friendly folks . . . I guarantee!

✦ ✦ ✦

GRAB A CAMERA . . .

Take action shots of men at play. Most guys will be thrilled that you're interested in getting some good shots of them. And be sure to get their name and number, so you can contact them later and pass on any good photos you've taken of them. And, of course, you can always set up another time to get together and snap more pictures. The more reasons you can find to be around them, the better it is.

✦

Find architectural building elements to shoot. Spend time doing this during lunch or for a few hours after work. Juxtapose buildings with surrounding scenery and ask a nice looking gentlemen if you can snap his picture in the foreground. Not only will he be flattered, but you can contact him again to give him a copy . . . that is, if you got his business card!

✦

Create a coffee table book. Pick a theme that relates to men, such as males and their cars, and go wherever there are opportunities for photographing your subject. Believe me, you will meet dozens of nice eligible bachelors doing this!

✦

Snap photos of dogs with their male owners. Who can't help but love you when you capture a really good shot of them with their best friend!

✦ ✦ ✦

VISIT A HOTEL . . .

Visit a hotel for an afternoon or evening. As you can probably tell, this is another of my favorite activities where you will have many occasions to meet lots of different people. But you'll see . . . once you get there!

✦

Reserve a table for lunch or dinner. Many of the larger hotels have several eateries, so pick one that looks good and enjoy yourself. And remember, you can always ask the host or hostess to seat someone who is dining alone at your table. Don't forget to check the lounge, they often serve bar food and you can bet there will be lots of fellows there, too!

✦

Snuggle into a cozy chair by a roaring fire in the lobby. This is a neat way to interact with guests especially in hotels where the fireplace is a focal point.

✦

Sip on a hot buttered rum in the lounge. What better way to spend a blustery day. And my guess is there will be others doing the same!

✦

Enjoy live entertainment later in the evening. Almost all larger hotels have something going on at night, either live music or dancing. So, stick around and see what you find. Besides, what else are you doing?

✦ ✦ ✦

AT THE BOOKSTORE OR LIBRARY . . .

Spend time in the library during the day. As mentioned previously, many public libraries, particularly those near commercial districts, are filled with men during the workday. Find a reason to spend a few hours there next week and situate yourself in the business section. This is where the men will be . . . and so should you!

✦

Read up on a public company you might be investing in at some time. Check archived information for news articles on companies or product trends. You will always find some fellow doing the same and I'm sure he'll be glad to show you how to start your search.

✦

Find a comfortable chair and read a magazine. Many gentlemen spend several hours every day at the library, reading the daily paper or a favorite periodical. There are numerous special interest publications available, including back issues, giving you a chance to read up on all sorts of male topics, such as the out-of-doors, sporting news and the high-tech industry. If there is a fellow nearby and you don't understand something you're reading, ask if he can explain it to you.

✦

Spend time at a medical library. Many doctors will be there reading up on medical problems and/or treatments during the lunch hour, early evenings, or weekends. Most major universities have medical libraries where you can stay current on health news or get information on some problem you would like to know more about. And, of course, you can always ask a gentleman to explain a term you're not familiar with.

✦

Go to a law library at the courthouse or a nearby university. Attorneys spend a lot of hours researching case precedent and other legal matters. And the best time to visit with them is when they are taking a break.

✦

Browse through the computer books. I have yet to be in this section and not chat with some fellow about different applications or what's going on with the Internet. And while you're at it, maybe he can help you find a good book for beginning website creation.

✦

Spend an evening at a bookstore . . . often overlooked as a place to meet men. Many are promoting themselves as a social focal point, where you can linger over a good novel, listen to an evening lecture series, or sip on a cup of coffee and chat with someone. It certainly merits checking out!

✦ ✦ ✦

RAINY DAY SCHEDULE . . .

Those of you who live in wet areas of the country understand the problems of getting out when the weather is inclimate. The following section offers a few ideas for meeting men even in a torrential downpour.

Hit the coffee bars . . . a latte and a friendly conversation on a rainy day may be the one suggestion that works for you!

✦

Go roller skating . . . in a covered parking structure near a professional building or high-tech company. You will likely find accountants, attorneys and programmers, who will be working during the evenings and on weekends to meet deadlines. And I'll bet one of them will have something to say when you bump into him as he is leaving for the day!

✦

Try bowling a game or two. Lots of men enjoy this sport which they can do no matter what the weather is like outside. This by far is one of my most favorite rainy day activities. Make it yours, too!

✦

Take a few laps in the pool . . . particularly at an athletic club or community pool during adult sessions. You might also look for masters programs at local swim clubs, where you can compete with other individuals in your age group. Not only is this a great way to meet men, but it will keep you physically fit.

✦

Spend an afternoon at the airport watching people coming and going. Talk with fellows who are waiting in the terminal or visit with individuals in one of the lounges or restaurants. This is a fantastic way to meet lots of men . . . but until you've tried it, you won't know that!

✦

Hang out at the private club you belong to. Use this time to get to know other members. You're paying for it, so you might as well use it!

✦

Whatever you do, don't stay at home. This is a good time to try one of the many suggestions you've been given . . . and if not now, when?

✦ ✦ ✦

SPECIAL EVENTS . . .

Go to a local event. Contact Chambers of Commerce, Visitor Centers, or check local newspapers for upcoming activities, like fairs and festivals, music concerts, or rodeos. The more male-oriented the event, the better for you. Clearly, you're not going to find many guys at Christmas shows and craft fairs, so don't go to them when you're looking for men. **$** Seek out functions, such as culinary or wine festivals, where affluent individuals will travel some distances to be there, then you can be assured it will be worth your time.

✦

Participate in a wine tasting. Many wine merchants and some restaurants frequently hold wine samplings and is a great way to meet their loyal customers, many of whom are single men. Ask to be placed on their mailing list so you can stay well-informed about these events . . . you don't want to miss out!

✦

$ Bid on a Cabernet Sauvignon at a wine auction. These sales will bring out the well-heeled connoisseurs, but read up on your vinos prior to the event, as you will want to know about Bordeaux wines before talking with someone. Contact local wine merchants for more information.

✦

Find out when local or state firefighter contests are held. Oftentimes you will hear about friendly competitions between several different city fire departments. Once you find out when and where . . . be there! The place will be swarming with cuties.

✦

Spend the day at a chili cook-off. You'll find lots of men at these events, both as preparers and tasters. The cooks pride themselves on their prize-winning stews, so don't miss an opportunity to get them to divulge their secret ingredient. Be sure to get there early and stay late . . . you don't want to miss anything!

✦

$ Go to a horse or livestock auction. These events may last several days and attract many wealthy breeders and cattlemen from all over the country. Be sure to frequent hotels, restaurants and other nearby establishments that stockshow goers will patronize during their stay. Affluent gentlemen are also attracted to thoroughbred race horse sales, so when you find out one is being held . . . get there as fast as you can!

✦

Go to a weekend art festival. Visit with male artisans – they will be in the booths featuring sculpture, woodworking and pottery. Pick up one of their business cards, so you can visit their shop at another time and continue the dialog.

✦

$ Join a walking tour of local art galleries . . . and put yourself in a position to meet men who have good taste and money. Many art communities will feature these art walks one evening a month . . . so, make sure you're a part of it, too!

✦

$ Attend a gallery opening . . . and come in contact with many artisans and gallery patrons. Opening nights are often by invitation, so be sure you're on their mailing lists . . . you won't be disappointed.

✦

Take a tour of a special military event. Anytime there is a naval vessel, aeronautical, or other special showing that is open to the public, don't miss it. There will be lots of gentlemen around, not to mention all the boys in uniform!

✦

Look for activities sponsored by fraternal associations . . . even though these organizations are for men only, they put on many functions that the general public may attend. Call your local Elks or Moose Hall to find out about upcoming events.

✦

Sit with a group of fellows at a pancake breakfast. This is a fun community event and usually one of the local men's groups will be doing the cooking. So, there is bound to be some of their buddies there, too. And, of course, you'll want to be around when they show up!

✦ ✦ ✦

TAKE A CHANCE . . .

If you notice several men driving down the road and they're wearing caps or visors . . . follow to see where they're going.

That is, if you have the time to give mad chase to complete strangers! Seriously though, they may be heading to the park, golf course, or some nearby area where you may get a chance to meet them. It's worth a try!

✦

Locate a long lost acquaintance. Have you ever wondered what happened to an old beau? Well, here's your chance to find him and see what transpires. You might be pleasantly surprised . . . wilder things have happened!

✦

Make a date with someone you've been admiring. How about that fellow you see in the elevator each morning? Why not ask him to join you for coffee or invite him to a party you're having. You know you want to . . . so do it! By the way, if he asks if he can bring someone to the party, don't assume he has a girlfriend. He just may be uncomfortable with a group of strangers and would like to have someone he knows with him. So, your response to him might be, "I was hoping you'd be with me."

✦

Place an ad in the Personals. I've known several women who have had success with this. But if you're like most of us, you are probably uncomfortable doing this on your own, so get several interested friends and do it as a group. Word the advertisement something like, "Several females, 35-45, looking for men in same age range to join us for dinner. Please contact . . ." Chances are those who respond will also have several single buddies who may be interested in meeting with you and your friends.

✦

Answer an ad in the personals. Again, be careful, you don't want to open yourself to a bad situation. So, have him join you and several of your friends for a drink and ask him to bring along a couple of his bachelor pals, too.

✦

Take acting lessons or try out for a part in a play. There are many opportunities at the local level and maybe that next love scene with the leading man will be more than pretend!

✦

Rent a motorcycle and take off for the weekend. This is not for the timid, but I guarantee you will meet plenty of bikers while you're out and about. As with car clubs, there are lots of motorcycle groups out there, including Christian groups, senior clubs and more. Check with a motorcycle shop or go online for local club information. **$** This, also, is becoming an extremely popular sport with many celebrities and well-to-do individuals who want to get away from it all. This is one group of men you don't want to overlook!

✦

Get a friend to go to a topless bar with you. Don't laugh! Many businessmen spend their lunch hour at these establishments – the food is good and the entertainment, well, I'll leave that up to you to decide. Women generally do not go into these places, so you will definitely be noticed if you do!

✦

Spend the day at a nudest colony or nude beach . . . men are the main participants in this clothes-free environment. And I'll bet you won't have any problem meeting other free-spirited individuals. Contact the American Association for Nude Recreation at (800) TRY-NUDE for a nudist group near you. There are more than 50,000 members and many of them are unattached men.

✦

Take a nude cruise . . . such as Bare Necessities Tour & Travel in Austin, Texas, at (800) 743.0405. This outfit continues to grow steadily and currently has four boats, the largest holding more than 1,500 folks. If you've never tried it, you just might like it!

✦ ✦ ✦

JUST FOR FUN . . .

One important aspect of meeting men is having a sense of humor. Most people, including men, enjoy being around individuals who are having a good time. One way to have a man notice you is to draw attention to yourself. Here are a couple of ideas where you will not go unnoticed.

Disguise yourself and go where no one knows you. Put on a wig that makes you look totally different and go somewhere and be whoever you want to be! Besides, you are more likely to let loose if you know you will not bump into anyone you know.

✦

Try wearing a "Kiss me, it's my birthday" button . . . and see what happens!

✦

Wear "Groucho" glasses and have a little fun with people. These are those plastic glasses with busy eyebrows and a big nose with a mustache attached. Wear these in the park, on a commuter, or other spots where you will come in contact with people. Someone will surely want to meet such a fun person!

✦

Rent a costume and go out other than Halloween. This is something you will want to do with a friend or two. Not only will you attract attention, several people will want to know what you are celebrating and before you know it, you'll have several men around you!

✦

Learn a few magic tricks . . . and go to the park and entertain folks. You'll not only meet lots of individuals, but you'll probably make a few of them laugh. And there's bound to be someone who will notice . . . but you'll have to try it first!

✦

Participate in a parade. Be whimsical or silly – wear a costume, dress up your dog, ride a tricycle, or build a float and pull it behind you. Come on, life's too short to not enjoy it . . . and the best part is you'll meet lots of fun-loving individuals!

✦ ✦ ✦

15

FOR SENIORS ONLY

You've lived through a lot just to reach this point . . . you've experienced the joys of raising children, the sorrows of burying one or more of your loved ones and everything in between. And here you are in the prime of your life, all alone . . . what a dirty trick! You know you deserve better and not one of us would disagree.

But, unfortunately, as we grow older, not only do we get set in our ways, but finding eligible men becomes more difficult, especially as the number of available males over 65 declines. And many of you have given up, you think you are too old to find companionship. Wrong! You do not have to resign yourself to a life of loneliness. There is hope – it just requires a little more time and effort and a lot more creativity.

STAY ACTIVE . . .

This is not the time to be sitting at home by yourself. You should be out meeting people and participating in lots of activities and there are several reasons why this is important:

- First, staying active allows you to hone your social skills. As with any other activity, the more you practice, the more adept you become. Unfortunately, the opposite is also true – the less interaction you have with individuals, particularly men, the more your socializing atrophies.
- Secondly, the more active you are, the more friendships you develop . . . and you know where that will lead!
- And finally, but more importantly, should anything unforeseen occur and one of the male members in the group finds himself alone, he will not have to leave this inner circle to look for a new companion . . . he will already have developed a rapport with you!

IT'S NEVER TOO LATE . . .

Shortly after I started jogging, there had been much ado in the newspapers about the upcoming Houston Marathon, as that particular year was one of the largest ever staged and runners from all over the world were participating. But what caught my eye, was the mention of the oldest runner in the race, a woman in her late sixties, who had just taken up the sport a few years earlier and was running her first marathon.

Knowing the hard work it takes to be a runner and having struggled myself for months to just get up to three miles, I wanted to see this incredible woman, if for no other reason than to let her know I was rooting for her.

Long after the race had ended, long after it had gotten dark and long after most of the spectators and participants had gone home, this determined little lady was still running. Those of us remaining, cheered and urged her on, and bless her heart . . . she finally did it. She completed all 26.2 miles! I could only imagine the pride she must have had on those blistered old feet.

The point is, you are never too old to get involved in something new and that also means a new relationship. There is no reason you should not enjoy the benefits of having a man in your life.

LIGHTEN UP AND HAVE FUN . . .

Over my desk hangs a picture of an elderly, heavy-set woman wearing a baggy shift and a straw hat with plastic flowers adorning the top. She apparently has returned from the market and has placed her groceries on the ground near several discarded toys. Spotting an abandoned hula hoop, she has kicked off her thongs and is attempting to twirl the hoop around her waist.

What I love most is she evidently is unaware that anyone is watching. She saw an opportunity to have a little fun and she grabbed hold of the moment . . . and for no other reason than to please herself.

In other words, lighten up and have fun! I believe, as you get older, this is the secret to finding companionship. There must be something that sets you apart from the other forty-nine women who are looking for that one eligible bachelor. And this is what it takes – a zest for life, a flair for fun and a sense of humor.

My dear friend, Mitzi, had this. Even though she was well into her seventies, she was seldom without a man. How did she do it? She used her outgoing personality and charm to flirt with men at every opportunity – at the market, the mall, wherever and whenever she came in contact with one of them. It made her feel good, the men enjoyed it, and the bottom line . . . it worked!

Although I am still a few years shy of the senior years, thanks to Mitzi and other mature friends of mine, some of their secrets for meeting men, and a few of my own that I think may be helpful, have been presented in the following pages. Some ideas may sound familiar, but have been revised for application by those of you who are reading this chapter.

LIVING ARRANGEMENTS

Move to a retirement community . . . or some other senior complex. I know many of you may be going, "ugh!" But if you do the research, you will find not only do these "senior cities" offer amenities that attract active retirees, but they also have many organized activities for residents. Contrary to what you may think, a community of retired people does not mean a bunch of old fogies shuffling around!

✦

Relocate to a warmer climate. Florida, Arizona and Southern California attract droves of mature individuals. Not only is warm weather an advantage, but many of the communities are built around golf course resorts and offer many other activities for "the good life."

✦

Advertise for a male roommate. Any number of older men would love to share a home with a woman. In exchange for room and board he can help around the house or with odd jobs. It's a good tradeoff, plus you'll have a man around whenever you need him. Be explicit with qualifications, "Non-smoking, male roommate, over 65 needed to do odd jobs in exchange for room and board." Focus on men who are outgoing with a lot of interests, who will probably have many friends. As previously mentioned, you do not have to share your home with anyone until you find the right fit. Besides, you will probably meet so many interesting men that you will want to continue interviewing more of them, at least until you tire of having so many new gentlemen in your life! Nevertheless, before interviewing anyone or giving them your address, check out their references and then meet them for the first time in a neighborhood coffee shop and be sure to bring a couple of your friends or family members with you.

✦ ✦ ✦

MEET YOUR NEIGHBORS . . .

Put out a community newsletter. This is a great way to get to know your neighbors, as you visit with each one and discuss any issues or concerns they may have, future articles and what specialty group(s) they may have an interest in. If you have a computer, it will make this a lot easier to put together and distribute.

✦

Interview a gentleman for your community newsletter or a local publication. You can spend several evenings finding out about him, and vice versa. If he's pretty special, you will want to drag this out as long as possible. Besides, once you get to know him better, anything can happen!

✦

Sit outside and visit with your neighbors. This is a great way to meet others who live nearby. And once you get to know one of the gentlemen that passes by each day, invite him to join you for a lemonade.

✦

Invite your neighbors for an informal get-together. Do something quick and easy, like welcoming a new male tenant or having a potluck where everyone brings something to eat or drink. If you are the "party gal," then everybody will want to know you, so they can be included in your numerous affairs, too.

✦

Find a few neighbors for a special interest club. Again, the more male-oriented the group, the more men will want to participate. A few ideas:
- *Card or game club* – such as Bridge, Pinochle, Cribbage, or Chess.
- *Travel adventures* – for weekend and vacation getaways.
- *Computer users* – exchange freeware or help each other with software and hardware problems.
- *Exercise group* – for daily walks and aerobic workouts.

✦

Take some "leftovers" to a male neighbor . . . like cookies or a casserole. I'm sure the few bachelors who live in the neighborhood are inundated with food from well-meaning women, but remember, it's your fun-loving nature and outgoing personality that is going to win him over . . . not to mention your good cooking!

✦

Help a charity. Go door-to-door asking for contributions and meet your neighbors while you help a worthwhile organization. Plus, this is a great way to introduce yourself to some of the gentlemen in the neighborhood you have not yet met. If you come across someone of interest, be sure to get his number so you can include him in your next function.

✦

Extend a dinner invitation for a particular night. Invite a few male neighbors and/or put up notices around your complex, for example, "Join me for homemade spaghetti every Tuesday at 5:30 p.m." Now all you have to do is make plenty of pasta and wait for the gentlemen to come by!

✦ ✦ ✦

LEISURE ACTIVITIES

HOBBIES . . .

Get involved with scale model clubs. You'll find the greatest number of older adults in groups specializing in trains, boats and airplanes. And since very few females are interested in model building, you will be one of a select few who gets to be in the company of these fellows.

✦

Find a group of older men flying model airplanes. This is a very popular pastime for many retired pilots. Look in parks, football fields and other open spaces or check with hobby shops and model airplane clubs for their whereabouts. Also, there are more than a thousand shows around the country. Anytime you hear about one, you had better be there . . . you'll be pleasantly surprised at what you find!

✦

Attend a model train show. Whatever you do, don't miss out on this opportunity to meet lots of gray-haired fellows. You will see numerous Lionel and HO-scale layouts which the owners have spent countless hours creating. As you walk around, stop and talk to these artisans about their creations . . . they'll talk your ear off!

✦

Visit a coin shop. Men continue to be the main purchasers of rare coins and many of them have been doing this for some time. While there find out when the next local coin show will be held . . . you won't want to miss it!

✦

Start a hobby of male collectibles. Many retired collectors will frequently be seen at specialty stores, antique shops, garage sales and swap meets looking for treasures. Anything having to do with the following, will bring out these collectors:

- *Trains, airplanes, boats and automobiles*
- *History* – particularly war memorabilia
- *Sports* – trading cards and autographed mementos
- *Guns and knives*
- *Tobacco pipes*

✦ ✦ ✦

GAMBLING . . .

Spend an evening at a gambling casino. This is a wonderful opportunity to be around people of all ages and have fun at the same time. In addition to many of the well-known destinations, don't overlook casinos on Indian reservations and locations across the border in Canada. Once you get there, try some of the suggestions on pages 88-90, *"They Are Gamblers."*

✦

Take a charter trip to a gambling spot. Cheap air and bus fairs to Las Vegas, Reno and other gaming spots are popular with seniors. Check the travel section of your Sunday paper or with your travel planner for availability. Although most participants are women and retired couples, once at the destination there will be plenty of fellows to choose from.

✦

Spend an afternoon at the horse races. Men probably outnumber women ten to one at the track, and during the week the number of elderly males soar. If you've ever wondered where these old-timers go during the day . . . this is where you'll find them! If you sit in the grandstands, there will be lots of fellows to visit with between races. **$** And, of course, the more affluent individuals will be in the Clubhouse or Turf Club. If there's a track nearby, go and see what I mean!

✦ ✦ ✦

COMPUTERS AND THE INTERNET . . .

Take a computer class. Seniors are filling up the classrooms in record numbers as they learn PC basics at night school. Although moving into the computer generation may be a difficult transition for many of you, don't find yourself left behind. Once you learn the basics, the whole world will be available to you!

✦

Get online. Older Americans are one of the fastest growing segments on the Internet and there are a large number of senior sites offering a variety of products, services and information. Just key in "seniors" and you'll be amazed at all you find!

✦

Create a personal website . . . include things you are fond of, your interests and any other pertinent information you'd like to share and then link it to one or more of the senior sites. You'll have no control over who contacts you, but you will have the opportunity to communicate with individuals all around the world. *Warning: do not be in a hurry to get together with those you may have a rapport with. Unfortunately there are a number of unsavory characters out there that will use their anonymity to prey upon unsuspecting senior citizens. Under no circumstances should you give out any personal information. Any meetings should include family or friends and be in a public place.*

✦

Register with an on-line dating service. There are many websites on the Internet that will pair up seniors with similar interests. A few offer this as a free service, but most charge a fee. With the influx of seniors online, there are many opportunities that are available. Please heed the previous warning, you don't want to find yourself in a difficult situation.

✦

Join a computer user's group. Men far outnumber the women in this crowd, especially Macintosh™ groups. With the increase in computer use by seniors, you are bound to meet many older gentlemen who can help you solve many of your PC problems. Contact local computer stores for more information. Even if you are not a computer user, I suggest you go to the meetings . . . you'll be glad you did!

✦ ✦ ✦

OTHER SPECIAL INTERESTS . . .

$ **Find a car show to attend.** You will find many seniors exhibiting their classic automobiles at weekend club showings or vintage auto exhibits. They've spent a lot of time and money restoring these beauties and love talking about them, so start the conversation by asking how long he's been working on his gem. You can spend all day walking around admiring them . . . both old autos and their owners!

✦

$ **Join the Classic Car Club of America.** There are chapters throughout the country and members are primarily over 50 and have lots of money, as these are not inexpensive automobiles.

✦

Get involved in bird watching. This sport is very popular with the older set. It's not very expensive to do and you will get a little exercise at the same time. All you need is a good pair of binoculars and a field guide to keep track of the birds you find. With over 800 species in No. America and 9,000 worldwide, this pastime will not only get you out and about locally, but also traveling around the country or the world, as well. But even better, you're going to love the people you meet!

✦

Join the Audubon Society . . . and attend regularly scheduled meetings, where you will get together with other bird watchers and share information. Many chapters are very active with frequent activities and outings. Give it a try and see what you think!

✦

Busy yourself with politics. This is a wonderful way to meet people of all ages and backgrounds, as you lend support to a favorite candidate at the local, state, or federal level. You might also want to consider getting on a civic committee or joining a community group. You will meet more people than you can imagine at numerous social, political and fund-raising events.

✦

Attend a tea dance or other ballroom dancing affair. Lots of elderly people enjoy this pastime and there will always be a couple of unattached gentlemen who will make sure all of the ladies have their turn on the dance floor.

✦ ✦ ✦

LEARN SOMETHING NEW . . .

Go through the Master Gardening program. Many male gardeners, especially retirees, are committed to this program. It's paid for by public taxes, so anyone can use their services. Contact your county extension for more information and requirements. However, be prepared to give back to the community by volunteering your time at nurseries and home centers to help gardeners with their plant problems. The best part, is you will come in contact with numerous men, both during the program and later when interacting with the public.

✦

Participate in a T'ai Chi class. Many seniors enjoy this unaggressive, spiritual form of martial arts and can continue to do so as they age, as it is less stressful on the body, with slow and deliberate movements that focus on "centering" oneself. It is extremely popular in the Orient and seniors fill city parks throughout the day as they go through their daily routines.

✦

Teach a subject. If you have some expertise, offer to teach a class at night or on the weekend at a senior center. Put up flyers at retirement complexes and other places seniors frequent or contact organizations for the elderly to set up a class schedule. A few ideas include cooking, dancing, Bridge, stained glass, typing, or computer classes.

✦

Offer a course for men only . . . like light cooking for one, gardening, computer basics, or Bridge. Here's an opportunity to have a captive audience of retired gentlemen . . . what more can you ask?

✦ ✦ ✦

GROUP INVOLVEMENT . . .

Get involved in a local Senior or Adult Day Center. Contrary to popular opinion, these are not filled with decrepit old people. Instead you will find active individuals who have a lot of interests and knowledge to share. There are numerous activities and trips, planned specifically for seniors, like dancing, bowling, sculpting, card games and more. In fact, you'll find it is more like an educational campus than an old folks home.

✦

$ Join a yacht club. There are a lot of old salts that belong to these clubs. If you like being on the water, this may be just the thing for you! In addition to sailing activities, clubs offer full-service restaurants and many social events. If you have the wherewithal . . . this will be money well spent!

✦

Spend time with a senior singles group. You'll find a majority of the members will be female, but that's okay, as it beats sitting at home alone. However, if the emphasis is on activities, like sporting events, fishing and gambling, there will be a lot more fellows participating. If you are unable to find such a group, start your own and advertise the fact, "Men over 60 wanted for active singles group. Activities include golf outings, a day at the race track and box seats at a local baseball game. For more information, please contact . . ."

✦

Join a special interest club. Seek out those that older men will be attracted to, which means you will not find many of them in sewing circles or flower clubs. If you stick to themes like sports, finances, airplanes, trains and automobiles, you'll find plenty of old gents.

✦

Get involved with Kiwanis and Rotary clubs. Many retired men are members. (No longer exclusively for males, as membership has opened up to females in recent years.) Not only is this a great social opportunity for you, but these groups do a lot of community service work. They meet on a regular basis and new members are always welcome. Do yourself a favor and go to the next meeting . . . it may change your life forever!

✦

Participate in a Probus group. Membership consists of Rotarians and offers fellowship for compatible individuals with similar backgrounds and is another good reason to be a part of this service group.

✦

$ Watch the stock market quotes at a brokerage firm. Most have areas for customers to observe Wall Street activity and you'll find many serious investors enjoying this pastime, especially older, well-off gentlemen.

✦

Start or join an investment club. These clubs pool together members monies to make investments the group has researched and decided to participate in. Many investment clubs are predominately female, so ask up front who are members. If you start one, gear it to retired males.

✦

Join a speakers bureau. This is for those of you with a motivational message you'd like to share or who are knowledgeable on a particular subject. This organization finds local groups that may be interested in your keynote speech. This will put you in contact with many people at different speaking engagements. Many retirees have a lot to offer and this is a wonderful way to share your knowledge and earn some added income at the same time.

✦

Look into "Loners on Wheels" . . . a recreational vehicle club for singles with chapters throughout the U.S., Canada and Mexico. It is open to all unmarried individuals, but mainly people over 60 participate. There are more women than men, but for those who love RV life and the comradery of like-minded seniors, this may be perfect for you!

✦

Busy yourself with Toastmasters. This is a public speaking group which meets weekly and helps each other perfect their communication skills. Many older men are members and lend their expertise to younger speakers.

✦

Get together with a group of men at a chess club. Check with senior groups and game stores for information on local gatherings. Also, look for older gentlemen playing in the park. This is a favorite way for many of them to spend a few hours during the day.

✦

Join a Bridge group. Bridge is a popular pastime with older retirees. If you want to start a group, advertise for singles only. There are lots of people out there who would love to play, but don't have a partner.

✦ ✦ ✦

THEY HELP OUT

Participate in a retired seniors volunteer program . . . such as SCORE (Service Corps of Retired Executives). This is sponsored by the Small Business Administration and is a business counseling service. Retired executives and entrepreneurs volunteer their time and expertise to small businesses in the community. Very few women are involved in this program and if you have any background in this area, it will be a wonderful opportunity to meet other volunteers and small business owners in your locale.

✦

Help out at a shelter. Offer to assist with food preparation or teach someone a skill, like how to type or use a computer. You will meet plenty of men and although they may be down on their luck, once they learn a new skill, it won't be long before they may have something to offer. So, don't rule anyone out!

✦

Volunteer to help out at a hospital. This is a great opportunity to meet all those men who are either there for medical reasons or visiting a friend or family member. Your kindness and friendliness may be all it takes to snag someone special!

✦

Offer free haircuts to men at the senior center. Not only is this a fun way to meet fellows, they may be so indebted for the freebie that they'll take you out dancing some night!

✦

Find out about self-help and support groups. Men generally do not attend these, but there are exceptions. As people age, cancer, Alzheimer's and bereavement programs will have many more elderly participants. You can always check with the sponsoring agency to find out what the group makeup is like. The main advantage is while lending support to each other, you have the possibility of getting to know an individual really well.

✦

Help an older man . . . with house cleaning, cooking, gardening, etc. And while you're there, spend some time getting to know him better.

✦ ✦ ✦

Recreation

Take up golf. This is a sport that can be played well into your senior years and is extremely popular with retirees. According to the National Golf Association there are 6.5 million golfers over the age of 50. Based on the older men I've seen on the course, this probably is the number one active sport for males over the age of 65. Even if you do not play, it's never too late to start. Try some of the suggestions on pages 105-109, *"Get Involved In Golf,"* you won't regret it!

✦

Visit a public golf course. The best times to go are early morning weekdays when older retirees are heading out to the links and men's days (one or two mornings a week reserved for the exclusive use of the men's group). And, of course, weekends will always be very busy. If you do nothing else, at least have lunch in the clubhouse and see what you think!

✦

Join a seniors golf group. Many public and private courses have men's and ladies clubs and a large proportion of the members are retirees. If you'd like to improve your odds of meeting eligible gentlemen, I suggest you get involved as soon as possible!

✦

Observe a senior men's tennis tournament . . . through the parks and recreation department or at a local racquet club. Actually, *any* senior men's event is worth watching, but you've got to get there first!

✦

Join a tennis club. Many seniors and the affluent belong to racquet clubs. Next to golf, this is probably the second most popular sporting activity for older men.

✦

Watch an evening men's slo-pitch game. Many city parks and recreation departments offer senior leagues (55 and over). When you add up the number of players on each team, plus substitutes, we're talking about several dozen gentlemen in one place! Once you find out when they're scheduled to play, get there as fast as you can! By the way, don't overlook Little League games, many grandfathers enjoy watching their grandchildren play.

♦

Join a fitness club. A lot of health club participants are over 55 and the best part is not only will you be improving your odds of living a longer and healthier life, but you will be meeting others who are doing the same. Check with local clubs to find out the best times to be around others in your age group.

♦

Participate in the National Senior Games. This is for anyone over 50 and is growing into a huge annual event with over 10,000 contestants competing in 18 different sports, including basketball, archery, swimming and track and field contests. You will also find many local and state competitions throughout the year. If there is not a chapter in your area, see about setting one up. For those of you who do not want to participate but would still like to be a part of this, volunteers are always needed to help at each event. And, of course, you can always spectate and cheer your favorites to the finish line.

♦

Get involved with orienteering. This sport – land navigation around a defined course with the aid of a map and compass – is one that many elders have an interest in. You can be as competitive as you want – either taking your time and enjoying your surroundings or finishing quickly by running over the varied terrain. The sport is timed, open to all ages and usually covers a 1-3 mile long course. For more information contact a chapter near you or write the U.S. Orienteering Federation, Box 500, Athens, Ohio 45701.

♦ ♦ ♦

TAKE A WALK . . .

Take a walk along the seashore. Early mornings and evenings are especially popular with the older set. Make a day of it – pack a lunch, bring a book, some music if you like, a blanket, your camera

. . . and enjoy yourself as you look for unusual rocks or gnarled driftwood.

✦

Go for a stroll around a mall. Mallwalkers are frequently seen before the stores open. This is great for those of you who are fearful of walking alone or when the weather is less than desirable.

✦

Stroll around your neighborhood . . . and visit with neighbors you don't know. And if you come upon a new gentleman on the block, be sure to invite him to one of the many functions you will be going to. Because if he's not right for you, he may be for someone else!

✦

Find a walking group . . . like Volkssport. This is a national group with chapters throughout the country. Members are generally older adults and gather for walks on a regular basis.

✦

Grab a leash and walk your dog. This is a great way to get to know who lives in your neighborhood. If you don't own a pooch, maybe you should consider getting one, not only will it be a wonderful companion, but if it's cute, people will come up to you and want to pet it. You might be surprised at the introductions you'll receive as a result of your new little friend!

✦ ✦ ✦

FISHING AND WATER ACTIVITIES . . .

Hook a marlin on a charter fishing trip. Deep sea and sport fishing charters are very popular with men of all ages. Be prepared to get up early and spend the better part of the day fishing. If you enjoy being out on the water and having a bunch of men around, you'll love this!

✦

Go fishing off a pier or dock. Lots of retired gentlemen enjoy doing this and if you have access to this mode of fishing, it is a good way to spend an early morning. If you'd rather not fish, you can always walk around the pier and talk with fishermen who are wandering about.

✦

Join a fly fishing club or some other angling group. You will find plenty of fellows and very few gals. If you like to fish and want lots of older gents to choose from . . . you'll enjoy this!

✦

Have breakfast at a café near a marina. Fishermen and boaters will be out early and the chances are very good they'll stop to get something to eat first. If you do this regularly, you will meet a lot of old salts.

✦

Sit outside a restaurant overlooking a marina and watch the activity. At the end of a long day on the water, many folks will want to relax out on the deck, too.

✦

Be part of a masters swim program . . . through the parks and recreation department or an athletic club. This is a wonderful way to stay in shape and meet other physically fit gentlemen.

✦ ✦ ✦

TRAVELING

Become part of a travel group. Plan weekend getaways, ocean cruises and European holidays. If you are forming a group, have in mind the first trip's destination and gear it to something men are interested in to assure that they will want to join. Then advertise: "Travel group forming for singles over 60, first trip is a golf vacation in Hawaii, future trips include a weekend in Las Vegas and exploring the ruins of the Incas." You can also get on the Internet and find even more senior travel opportunities.

✦

Participate in an Elderhostel program. This is a fabulous chance for those over 55 to meet people, travel and take part in any one of more than 2,000 learning environments. Over 250,000 participants, mainly retirees from 55 to 80, are enrolled in classes each year and it also provides a way for solo women to travel and not have to worry about personal safety. Contact Elderhostel at (877) 426-8056 or write them at P.O. Box 1751, Wakefield, MA 01880.

✦

Find a travel companion. Contact your travel planner or go online and discover many organizations that offer this service. And when you're not traveling, perhaps you can share the knowledge you've acquired about your community and be a companion to tourists coming to your locale. Just think of all the people you'll meet!

✦

Go to a golf school. Now that many seniors have time to perfect their golf swings, they are attending these instructional schools in large numbers. Located in warm climates in the South and West, you will find lots to do, even if you are not a golfer.

✦

Invest in a timeshare . . . at a retirement or golf resort. Need I tell you there will be plenty of gentlemen there? Focus on areas that are noted for having a lot of retired people, like the Palm Springs area, Florida and Arizona.

✦ ✦ ✦

SERENDIPITY

Contact ex-colleagues, neighbors, school chums and other friends you've lost contact with. You never know what someone's status is – people get divorced, spouses die. You often hear these wonderful stories about old lovers who were reunited after fifty years. Maybe one of them can be you!

✦

Sit in on a trial at the county courthouse. You often see older women sitting in the courtroom knitting, as they listen to civil and criminal cases. This sure beats sitting at home watching soap operas, plus you have the potential of meeting many of the men who are there for various reasons. The snack bar will be a busy spot first thing in the morning and during recesses, which will give you an opportunity to discuss the case you're watching with someone.

✦

Spend time in the public library during the day. Many retired gentlemen can be found in the financial section, reading *Barron's* and the morning *Wall St. Journal*. Find yourself a seat nearby and see if one of them can help you with your stock picks. There's no harm in asking and he might turn out to be the best pick you'll make!

✦

Get a part-time job at a VFW or Moose hall . . . or other fraternal group. There are lots of old-timers here. So, find out what opportunities are available and see who you meet!

✦

Become certified as a tax preparer . . . and help seniors with their tax returns. Just about anyone can do this, look for classes through your community college or with a tax service franchise that trains their personnel. Not only will this bring in some extra income, but you'll get to know who is married and some idea of their assets. This could be the one idea that changes your life!

✦

And finally, sit with an older gentleman during "early bird" hours. At many restaurants, this is the so-called "seniors hour" and is a great way to meet men. Most fellows by themselves will be sitting at the counter, so follow Mitzi's advice and sit down next to one of them and introduce yourself. Do this on a regular basis and you won't be looking for a man much longer!

✦ ✦ ✦

AFTERWARD

Well, that's it! I've covered a lot of territory, but if just one of these suggestions helps you find the man you are looking for, then I've done what I set out to do.

I've led you to the wellspring and now it's up to you to snag the one you want. There are plenty of fish in the pond and you will catch one . . . if you are in the right place at the right time with the right attitude. And that, my friend, is the secret.

So, I will leave you with this parting thought: instead of being the woman who is looking for any man, become the woman any man is looking for . . . and you will succeed.

Additional copies of *"Where are the Men?"*
may be ordered from the publisher
or for quicker delivery,
visit our website at
www.wherearethemen.com

InData Group, Inc.
Book Dept.
1420 NW Gilman Blvd., Box 2313
Issaquah, WA 98027

425.881.6368 Voice
425.881.7135 Fax

$14.95 per book
plus $3.95 shipping and handling